Glimpses of Hope

Selected Poems by Michael Fitzgerald

Michael Fitzgerald is the author of numerous volumes of poetry, nonfiction, and children's literature and the winner of several awards. He is a Pulitzer Prize nominee and has studied at the Iowa Writers' Workshop. He has edited two anthologies on the arts, *Creative Circle* and *Where Art and Faith Converge*. He has worked on projects for the American Jazz Museum, the Association for Bahá'í Studies, the Folger Shakespeare Library, the National Endowment for the Arts, Sarah Lawrence College, Smithsonian Institution, the Virginia Commission for the Arts, the University of Michigan, and others. He lives and works in the Shenandoah Valley of Virginia.

Other Full-Length Volumes
BY THE SAME AUTHOR

Poetry

A Tree Like This   *The Holy Passions*
Living the Boundaries   *Anthems for Earth*
A New World Suite   *Work Songs*
God's Whimsy   *Sonata of Spirit*
Rhapsody   *A New Era Symphony*
Planet Dreams
Songs for the Phoenix

Nonfiction

At a Glance   *Solitude and Solidarity*
Notebook

Editing

Creative Circle (ed.)   *Where Art and Faith*
Earth Circles (ed.)   *Converge (ed.)*

Children's Literature

How to Live Sideways
Hooray for the Planet

Glimpses of Hope

Selected Poems by
Michael Fitzgerald

Acknowledgments

Many thanks to the following publications where some of these poems first appeared: *Poetry, Ploughshares, The Alaska Quarterly Review, The Atlanta Review and Paideia,* plus the chapbook presses: *Purple Rose Press, Rainbow's End Books, White Mountain Publications,* and *White Wings Press.* Special thanks also to May Hofman and George Ronald Publisher, who published *Songs for the Phoenix, The Holy Passions,* and *Sonata of Spirit;* to Justice St. Rain of Special Ideas; and to Anne Gordon Perry and Rhonda Palmer, who shared the work of editing and bringing this book to fruition; Tim Perry and Antonio Rojas, who contributed design work and elements; and Sherry Grey, my long-time assistant.

NINE PETAL PRESS

Cover photo *Dennis Grundman*
Book design *Jacob Harman*

ISBN-13: 978-0998425641
ISBN-10: 0998425648

www.NinePetalPress.com

*Dedicated to my brother John M. Fitzgerald
and my sister Virginia M. Fitzgerald*

Foreword

Many dabble in the writing and reading of poetry, but Mchael Fitzgerald immerses himself in it. Dedicated to his craft and poetic calling for five decades, with volumes of published poems and poetry prizes awarded his work, Fitzgerald proves himself a worthy poet. He is also a great editor, writer of prose, friend, and muse.

This volume brings together works spanning Fitzgerald's decades of writing and publishing. He has combed through his collection of polished jewels to choose the most brilliant and priceless among them to share. With a voice that is powerful, hopeful, universal in its perceptions and influences, sophisticated yet accessible, life-embracing, art-enhancing, and spiritually aware, he calls us to ponder the important—nay, essential—aspects of life.

Transformation—both individual and collective—is often Fitzgerald's theme. For example, one of his volumes of poetry is called *Songs for the Phoenix*—aptly named, since the phoenix is quintessentially associated with rebirth. In his work we find over and over an affirmative articulation of the possibility of self and societal recreation, not in a naïve sense but one informed both by the Bahá'í Revelation (a world-embracing religion positing the oneness of humankind, equality of the sexes, harmony of the races, balance of science and faith, inevitability of world peace, and importance of the arts) and his own insightful understanding based on observation, growth, and illumination.

Fitzgerald calls humanity to the arena of transformation, not just those who might be considered among the intellectually or artistically élite, or even those who have undergone the most suffering; he sees the "perfect phoenix / flying the dance of everyone— / . . . singing the earth's song." He includes references to workers, the disabled, carpenters, and composers— women, men, and children, for in his work there is a "seat at the table for everyone."

Fitzgerald also pays homage to known figures: Steven Hawking, Dostoevsky, Miles Davis, Dizzy Gillespie, Lawrence Ferlinghetti, Allen Ginsberg, Horace Mann, John Coltrane, and others, and to Bahá'ís such as Tahirih, Louis Gregory, Roger White, Doc Holladay, and Billy Roberts.

The journey this poet inspires relates to both the inner and outer experience of this life (including the "unspeakable dark") and the contemplation of worlds to come, as promised in religious texts. He acknowledges the chaos and troubles of this age, and at the same time points to a time beyond them, affirming the importance of saying "Yes!"— "yes to the future within the present,/ yes, to Bahá, to singing,/ yes to the inexorable drive toward peace." Even in addressing the presence of war and conflict, he remembers "the single cherry blossom." Looking to the future, he affirms, "I sing tomorrow."

Fitzgerald's images reflect the natural world as well as the numinous, celestial one as he explores "the deep unknown." He calls upon us to face "the big empty"—and therein find, among others things, "a new world, rising." He reminds us that "we must touch bottom and rise."

Though he addresses universal concerns, many of Fitzgerald's subjects, metaphors, and themes have special relevance for Bahá'ís. Some of the poems deal specifically with Bahá'í central figures and content, such as "Elegy for the King, Bahá," a reference to the Bahá'í Founder, Bahá'u'lláh. Some deal with specific Bahá'í Holy Days such as Ridván. Some references are more oblique but can be understood in light of Bahá'í symbols and metaphors—roses and nightingales, for example. "Roses are my chief concern," he writes in one poem, alluding to his commitment to the spiritual life. "Living the color crimson" is a phrase he uses to further illustrate this connection.

Fitzgerald relates to the Supreme Being in multi-faceted ways, bringing us closer to Him/Her. He writes of the "God of Whimsy" and of "a quirky God"; God as a "cosmic mechanic"; God as an artist who "tosses His paints across the sky every night"; God as a potter, shaping clay. He pleads with God to "dance with us at the new world café." He encourages us to know God as "Lover, Friend, Hero."

The poems often bring together what might be seen as opposing forces; art and religion are fused in Fitzgerald's work, "embracing like fire and air," and, he also says, "my mind is bent on the fusion of two lovers, science and religion." In the poet's view, the unity of all religions will be part of the "architecture for a new world." He calls for a greater balancing of male and female aspects and a respect for womankind, as well as for all races.

Peace is the dream and promised outcome when opposition turns to fusion. Fitzgerald envisions, "one day, a Parliament of Earth," and he describes "bending to hear and breathe the peace dream." Art, whether poetry, painting, music, dance, film, or architecture, is integrally interwoven in the dream of *this* peace.

Poets (and artists of all kinds) help us to make connections, envision new worlds, and nurture our individual and collective dreams, and Michael (here I switch to his first name, intentionally) has done this sublimely. For many of us, he has been our Muse, encouraging our own poetry, soliciting us to write essays for his collections, responding to our occasional bursts of creative productivity while he steadily worked on his.

On one occasion, after I had mailed Michael something I had written, he mailed back a single word: "Primo!"

And here I wish to say to him now, regarding the body of his heroic, excellent work and to his life as a Poet:
"PRIMO!"

Anne Gordon Perry
April 21, 2018

Contents

Foreword, *by Anne Gordon Perry* i

Selections from:
A Tree Like This *(1988)*

On the Day of Your Becoming 3
A Tree Like This 4
Capturing a Vision 6
Fine Lines 7
Hospitals 8

Living the Boundaries *(1989)*

The Road 15
Lexicography of a Café 16
Blue Ridge Love Song 17
Fitzgerald Men 18
Saxman 19
Testament 20
Leisure 20
Those Hands, That Face 21
Fixing It Yourself 22
Selma, Montgomery and the Army 23

New World Suite *(1990)*

Unity-Dancing 27
Living the Color Crimson 36

God's Whimsy *(1990)*

Latitudes of the Heart 47

In Sum 47

Breakfast 48

Numinous – Word, Lake and Power 49

God's Whimsy 50

Rhapsody *(1990)*

Selections 55

Planet Dreams *(1991)*

Shadow and Stone 63

Floating on the Edge 63

Transportation 64

Colorado Spruce 65

Night, Night Listen Well 65

Going to the Universe 66

Songs for the Phoenix *(1995)*

Midnight 69

Shades of Violet 70

A Poem of Friendship 71

Autumn Luck 72

The Origin of Singing 72

A New Rising 73

Oneness Wings 74

A Tincture of the Absolute 75

Letter to God
   for Roger White.. 76
A Surmise of Elegance...................................... 77
The Edge of the Galaxy 78
The Environmentalist
   for my brother 79
Outlandish Gratitude 80
Meditation 80
A Friend's Farm... 81
Canaveral Couplets.. 82
Nightingales and Roses.................................... 83
An Evening Performance 84
Diner Days.. 85
Gabriel Has Taken Wing
   for Dizzy Gillespie 86

The Holy Passions *(1998)*

The Holy Passions 89
Decibels 90
Report from the Edge 91
Divine Logic
   The Bahá'í World Centre 92
Haikus for Earth 93
A Clearing... 94
Christmas Vespers.. 95
Harbors of the Heart.. 96
Jo-Jo's Song 96
Changeless Light Upon Light 97
Bahá'í Cool
   for Billy Roberts 98
Outrageous Sweet Planet 99

The Church of the Big Blue Dome 100
Proud Sunset 101
The Question of a Mama 102
World Religion 103
Farvashi, Inner Light 104
Song for Jerusalem 105
Journey Poem 106
A Gathering in the Backyard 107
The Red Maple 108
Vortex
  The Martyrdom of the Báb 109
How Articulate, the Dead 110
The Dharma Café 111
Crimson Elegy 112
After Long Effort 113
Dust of the Heart 114
Shenandoah Song 115
Dreaming a New Velocity 116
Dreaming It New 116
Dancing at the New World Café 117
Night's Celebration 118
December Evening 119
The Master Is Gone Tonight 120
This River, This Thunder 121
Dancing at the Thorazine Hotel 122
We 123
Joy-Day
  The Birth of Bahá'u'lláh 124
Christmas Eve Canticle 125
Charleston Vignette 126
Shenandoah Vignette 127
She 128
To Honor a Titan 129
Skyscape 129

Song of Unity 130
A Light from Persia
    The Declaration of the Báb 131
Local Pottery and a Jamaican Band.............................. 132
The Smile, The Portrait.. 133
Elegy for the King, Bahá.. 134
Architecture for a New World 135
Peace Dream.. 136
Sentinels of Peace
    Wolfeboro, N.H. 137
The Roots of Jazz 138
Death and the Robe of Heaven 139
A Lover's Song... 140

Anthems for Earth *(2002)*

A Long Poem.. 143

Work Songs *(2004)*

Song for the Workers... 181
We, the Determined
    A Poem for the Disabled 182
On Light... 183
There Is a Seat at the Table... 184
Rock Musician with a Ph.D. 185
Handworks Gallery Vignette 186
Jazz Song... 187
World Music Medley 188
On Architecture 189
The Mind of God 190
God, the Potter 190
The Luck of Flight 191
Loading Dock Blues... 192

Sonata of Spirit (2005)

One Chord, One Song.. 195

River Song... 196

Meditation Hall... 197

The Colors of One Palette.. 198

The Heart's Own Currency and Cost
for Louis Gregory.. 199

Rosette
for the Bahá'í Women 200

Folk Song 201

Farming Meditation 202

Men's Song
for Dennis Grundman 203

Each Religion Is Larger than Itself 204

A Credible Distance 205

Report from the Tao 206

Kent State Memoir 207

Politics at a Distance 208

"More Universal than Thou" 209

Southern Moon 210

World Centre Vignette 211

For the Universal House of Justice................................... 212

Prophet, Prisoner, Man of Peace...................................... 213

To Learn and to Love... 214

On Einstein 215

Spading the Earth.. 216

A New World Song... 217

One Mosaic, One Mandala, One Home 218

Thunder, Dream and Harrow 219

A Lake in the Mind 220

The Landscape That is Not There
for Charles Wright.. 221

Chicago Song.. 222

Pin-Light Angels Amidst the Unspeaking Dark.............. 223
Of Evergreens and Snows.................................... 224
The New Hampshire Lakes Region 225
Witness 226
A History of Dreams.. 227
In the Dance.. 228
Why?.. 229
Tracings of Spirit 230
An Arts Suite 231
Ballot
    for Jeanie Bauserman 231
Buddhist Economics
    for E.F. Schumacher...................................... 232
Bookseller with Coffeehouse
    for Lorne Bair 232
Concert Zen 234
Kind of Blue
    Marvin "Doc" Holladay.................................... 235
Each Note a Pearl
    for my sister 236
To Play with Feeling 237
The Tao of Music 238
For Love of Writing.. 239
 The Uses of Art 240
Star-Road Universe 241
Soul Song 242
Elegy for the True Brother 243
Last Words.. 244
Another Way 245
A Sonnet of Hope 246
Glimpses of Peace... 247
Anyone, From Any Direction, Is Welcome Here 248
Go Deep 249
A Turn of the Clock... 250

What Purpose, Faith 251
Windows on Being 252

A New Era Symphony *(2014)*

Song of the Planet 255
The Global Becoming 256
Matisse and Picasso for an Hour 257
Global New Real 258
Renewal of Faith 258
Race Unity at Five 259
Green Poem 260
Peace Poem 261
Love Is the Way the World Opens 262
Mercy Blankets 263
On J.S. Bach 264
One with the Road 265
How Trees Vibrate 266
Logos and River 266
The Sound of the Human Voice 267

Note to Reader 269

From
A Tree Like This
(1988)

On the Day of Your Becoming

For a Friend

From a median point of the last compass
you took into the country,

the trees gave leaves and the sky wondered.
Interests became interests again

and theatre came to your ears with music.
Why became being and why not was your leader

in the 60s aura that never stopped living.
The simple resonance of your song clipped

the impossibility of the day into proportion
like the perfect hand of destiny sweeping

the weeds from your garden. Mixed, stirred,
penetrated, you became the person who could

guide a ship into a mined harbor, the man
who could turn his back on parallel fifths

and learn the becoming of seeing oneness
in a javanese gamelan. From there, dare I,

you leapt in the spring of the whole universe
with ecstasy like the spirit. It was, it was.

There in the heart of your afterthoughts, the jasmine,
you lingered like sage, parceled out for your days,

until clover became a mine for your digging.
The ferreting, undone diversity of it left you spinning,

but the ferocity of its reason came into you like fire.
It was to – not a not to – it is the person you are,

you have given yourself to the wisdom you have found
and back in New Hampshire there remain a lake and pines.

A Tree Like This

A perfect tree,
It is the New Buddha, the New
Totem. If there were no further reason
for this Tree's healing
it would be the substance of justice.
It comes of the readiness to see that war's
 red river of semiotic blood, the verifiable
evidence of our demise, is the sense
of intensity at the heart of trees
broken open with savage blows at life itself.
It is a particular tree, the re-invention
of the paradisical, the idea of humanity
as "the leaves of one tree,"* like the
capable and luminous in substantial form.
I am thinking of the credible,
the soaring lines of becoming,
the single point for the definition of eternity.

His roots, like the idea of a region
To the world, acquire their redolent reasons
of timelessness in the remembrance of Abraham
and the balm of Gilead. There, the crest
of ocean's waves are human highness
and the minor key of a Beethoven
grasps oppression in its place.
Then, the sound of innocence becomes
the wisping of the branches in the wind,
and the sight of this standard
in the garden itself
restores human intrinsic feeling.

Bahá'u'lláh

A perfect tree,
like the idea of trees or notes
in the mind of the first musician.
A measure of His human, actual form,
is the kindness of mothers,
and the patience of unenviable nature
in its glacial recovery from the hand
of human evil. I am working
on a feeling so praiseworthy that I will
offer it up at the mention
of this Tree, forty years hence
in my hopes of dying a good death.

The sky is His azure curve
in a cosmos as wide as things,
as plural as the first stone.
I have spent my life looking at trees
and have yet to see the furthest extent
of this Tree of Life. It is by the branches
of this Tree that I affirm the survival
of the human race in the nuclear age.
I am thinking of a cypress in Israel
as perfect as Buddha/as perfect as Christ.
Bahá'u'lláh, this Tree, the very reason
to reclaim religion in a time of Inquisitions/
the palatial heart I take to in my poverty/
the motive of languages/the Tree as primal Word/
a Tree like this.

Capturing a Vision

Because
you have come in view,
there surge a lake and waves,
the cusp and the apex peal
with an absolution and a promise
that wind will be at my back.

The freedom
of your embraces
new, rehearsed, known, affirmed,
quits me in the hollows of my perfect hands,
silence and a flowing fountain
comfort me until no longer
will the nearness nestle nor
the willow wisp.

O Untrammelled, Quicksilver
Friend, Fable in Sight, leave,
and be thou Gold! Stay,
and be thou Fire! Die
to Live and Come Thou Once
Forever!

Fine Lines

Does the architect in you thirst
for fine lines and complexity, elegantly
portrayed? Is there a quest in the garden
for the perfect drawing?

When my grandfather laid down his pen,
his father had been gone awhile, sketching sermons
over his son's shoulder for forty years.
The subject of generations precludes
excess of distinctions when
the chicken houses on the Massachusetts farms
include

porticos, gables and the minister of twelve
hiding in the hayloft
with Chaucer or was it Dante?
I never leave home without a note pad and pen.

Hospitals

I

The needle breaks the surface
in slow-soft precision
on a background of whole flesh.

I lean back to ponder
the mechanical love
as the nurse hits the hospital

bricks as soon as it is over.
Needle, bright and silver, out.
Projectile to the blood, gone.

I ease into sleep. Is it only
because I no longer hear her touch?
What ministry does the chemical perform?

Is it anywhere the potent medicine
of her dress, her arms touching me?
I am left. The window out onto the city
protects me from bleeding onto the floor.

II

"Christ" passes across some modern lips
like the metaphor of some idea
twice removed from the concept.

Still, the path to praises
traces down the one thing we know
for prayer – seeking the resonance of love

This wintered Name and His living legacy
cross paths in the hospitals
where moments of human speaking –
despite denominations,
despite encrusted dogmas –
say what it is we all long for.

The cancer patient – terminal –
who writes her own funeral –
as a Celebration;

The psych ward where someone
who thought he was God
accepts a piece of his own humanity;

The chaplain who dies a little
with the patient by admitting
to being scared about – what next – himself.

III

The especially sick especially cherish hope.
It is their strange and vital medicine
when medicine falters.

Life and death side by side –
one, bustling nurses,
the tonic of visitors,

youthful rebellions and adult competencies;
the other, clamoring for your submission
with dubious promises of peace –

you choose the first sometimes
only because you must –
your soul, though worn, will have it no other way.

Even sophisticates may subscribe to
the power of positive thinking with their
backs up against their own mortality.

IV

We are all plagued by half-hidden secrets
between the gray sighs under the covers
as they wheel by another stretcher –

Compassion hides them with poor memory –
and a smile – our muscles rest in smiling
and regenerate with laughter;

Prayers may be answered in a quick death;
or jogging or whirlpools –
much less the tossing aside of crutches at the altar.

Healing minds, hearts and bodies
is not the sole property of doctors or sects. It is the conjunction
of love and science.

I do not cross myself
except as a Hindu, Buddhist, Jew – Bahá'í – who found Christ
flat on my back.

V

Choose truth for love is its source
and the dominant note of the universe.
It will claim any situation of suffering

for its victory without regard to credentials.
The Christ legacy is lived out each time we choose to overcome
our smallness,

to realize the largesse of the Creator
of religions is available at each turn. . . .
Quietly, I enter the semi-private room and bow down,

Quietly, I realize that it is not so much
I who choose, but Him who heard my cry before I chose.

From
Living the Boundaries
(1989)

The Road

Back in the Shenandoah Valley, with work
like the threshing floor in a thorough farm,
to clarify in the concrete, to work on poems . . .
I remember a temperate wind
on Rt. 70,
windows in my Chevrolet wide open,
a steady sense of sailing right through Indianapolis
to Colorado,
there in the rising portals
of a half-spent moon,
that inland place.
A mid-dial rock'n'roll station
the Beatles/Steeley Dan/Paul Simon/
endless mercury vapor lamps coming up, endless.
One by one, along the span of farms, end to end,
like the bales of hay I had worked on the farm,
100 pounds over the shoulder and into the truck.
I closed my eyes and leaned my head back/running
like the freshness of the wind.
Put in a few dollars/a cup of coffee/driving one handed/
the road bent around my mind like the manuscript
envelope/the book I have become.

A constant tension envelope/song by song/
the big sky, large enough to keep
and give away out the side windows.
A round heart now, dark, maybe red enough
to close around the hart of rock'n'roll,
ten miles from Denver/winning the dark side
of the road, riding a messenger of joy/
thumping the wheel over the liberation of my rhyme,
the iconoclasm of it/exile and return/
an odyssey of passion.

Lexicography of a Café

A cafe is a purple place, sufficient
reason to breathe another breath,

a kind of reason for being,
like the road, or a mountain retreat

you can find in the city.
often enough, there are originals

on the walls – a French roast,
or cappuccino by the hour – tables outside –

and you can lose yourself
the way saints do in meditation

by going there late at night.
You can peer out at the street and wave

as your friends walk by within reach almost;
you can climb Jacob's ladder

in your reading as they come for a re-fill, or
you can disappear upstairs

into the Zen temple at Kyoto
as you sip some herbal tea –

it is almost illegal to go there
so you can take a look at the night sky

and see where Orion is before you go.
If you work a day job,

and paint evenings and weekends,
it is already known to you, perhaps

in the canvas you picked up in the street
from an old tent. Or maybe

the beauty of God's laughter
has led you there by the song

you have re-found
from twenty years ago,

this cafe, this place for eating destiny,
this overture to the moon.

Blue Ridge Love Song

I build an improvised wall –
fieldstone from these Blue Ridge foothills –
and form it around us.
A rush to the gate
to greet you surges in me
as the last light of evening
tumbles down the sky.
I slay your weariness
as you lay down my worry;
a lake of tenderness
leaps into our eyes,
as we speak. Laughter
is the shared food of our communion,
and we knit together our broken hearts
with wildflowers.

Fitzgerald Men

My brother and I sat down to dinner
at the Chinese place with nods to each other
as if we were there on business, barely met
an hour before. Gradually, boyish smiles
crept into our eyes and swept our mouths
as we realized the massive privilege,
the immense freedom that was ours –
an entire Friday evening, just us, just the men.
We spent a full twenty minutes, I think,
rehearsing Szechuan names and Kung Pao.
We ordered drinks for our wait,
then something happened in the dream
and we were walking through the city
after our meal, writing our own script
of an Irish folk singer and his friend.
John did get up on the stage to sing,
and I did talk to the girl
the whole time. "Resin the Bow," "The Old
Reuben James," "Isn't It Grand Boys,"
then midnight, then 1 A.M. The streets
became a reflection of our steps and
we merged with history, nodded
to each other again, and walked
across the night sky.

Saxman

A tenor sax in Jerry's hand stirred
the leaves in our town like
May breeze. He could ride the downbeat
at the edge of a tune straight through
to the end, like his own freight train
across the Plains. His mellow improvisation
put the band in a mood, and things
happened in his hands on that sax
that should not happen. The audience
invariably swayed when he played,
the drummer was a better drummer when he played,
the trumpets declaimed like kings.
The earth disappeared when he got up
into his notes, and the young sound we had
back in 1969 brooded way down until the lava
in us kicked up and shot to the jet stream.

Jerry had control that set you free
and walked across thruways sideways
without making you feel a single bump.
He made wars fade away and stood there
at six foot three inches and found ways to be humble.
When he stood up for a solo, nobody
in the band flinched, and the audience
leaned back for line, speed, and tone
like driving a Mercedes on the Autobahn.
Everything you wanted to happen, happened
with his rides, as we call them,
and when he sat down after sixteen bars,
the band rode out of town without looking back.

Testament

My life is to say "Yes!"
to the inner territory
and the outer journey.
It is to discover a place
to let go of the rage,
a place to simply let go –
it is
to recover from
the death of my angels;
it is to die well,
to live well, inside out.

Leisure

Time enough to think
remains an imperiled thing,
like a piece of pure
coastline,
or a night with only music.

I take myself aside
in the afternoon and nap;
and at the close of day
I weep my fill of
consolation
in the arms of Almighty God.

Those Hands, That Face

I watched Arthur Rubinstein play
at Constitution Hall, my senior year
in high school, when the master was over 90.
The face was the face of an angel;
the hands were glissandi in themselves.
My sister and I froze in attention
as we lost our fears in the immersion
in such quality, such excellence.
Breathless, we dared to take stage seats,
within a glance and a nod of his vision.
Two hands, hummingbirds leaping over one another,
wrapped up in the motion of their harmony,
lived like kings at the end of those arms.
The Steinway gave him a region fitting
that kingship, and the reach and range of the man,
like a prince as might become him, lordly,
swept decibels away from seeing, and lofty men
knelt to see the ivory sweep and lift.

Fixing It Yourself

My father worked as a labor mediator
in Texas during the forties. It was election time

and the Sheriff and his deputies
had commandeered the voting box

to make sure the union didn't win and
certainly, to make sure none of those so-called

undesirables, blacks and hispanics, could vote.
Unarmed, only one hundred and forty pounds,

but 6'1" and duty in his blood
from night flights in World War II,

the Irishman heard about this at his office,
and walked into the place.

He gave the Sheriff and his men
three options – dealing with a Federal law suit,

the hospital or both –
an hispanic man who had been told to leave

turned around and came back to vote
as the Sheriff and his boys got up to go.

Today at sixty-seven and retired, a minister/social worker,
a word from my old man will still cost you your excuses,

and I know middle-aged men
who go to him, as I do,

when they want a straight story,
the prospects for their own bloody histories,

a skeleton key to the Father's House,
a cosmic mechanic you can trust.

Selma, Montgomery and the Army

The orchards over the hills from my parents house
were full with apples and peaches when my father and I

climbed over the hill to get there, my first time home
from college. He looked up at the sky

as if trying to read the clouds or tell by the moon,
which had come up above the horizon to thirty-five degrees
        or so.

I remember him saying he was happy
after leaving the parish ministry and going into social work.

I could still feel the red breaths
of a Bronx streetfighter as we walked

through the foot-deep hay—his broken nose from the war
and the jeans I wore came under the sway of the moon

and we decided to turn toward the fallow fields
next to the orchard. As we stood there, finally,

on the top of those Blue Ridge foothills,
he told me about desegregating the mess in the army.

Him a mere sergeant, seeing black soldiers
forced to sit outside in the mud to eat their C-rations—

storming inside with his .45 unflapped
to tell Major Weimer that he had better

get those American soldiers out there
a decent place to eat—inside—

side by side with the rest, or
he would have an angry sergeant to deal with—

as the Major went outside to invite the soldiers in to eat,
my father joined a table of Texans to make sure of his back.

I drove back to Connecticut that night
like the reflection of a star, hoping for northern lights on
        the way.

From
New World Suite
(1990)

Unity-Dancing

I

As the community of nations
struggles on a whirling horizon
we go to the China
we have come to know and
speak tenderly, forcibly, embraces
to the Soviet-Self
we have left behind –
a friend in the Gulag,
unsung, unbidden to our table.

I go then,
to sing this circle of the sky,
shadow and light,
light upon light,
working out the roses of the Talmud,
the perfume of Allah, Yahweh, Brahma,
and the cafe I linger in is its own place
in the mind.

II

The quest for peace
beyond this account of war
we read in the news,
leans into the outline
of a century of the Hague,
the League of Nations,
the United Nations,
one day, a Parliament of Earth.

There comes an energy
akin to beauty
as the decline of beauty runs head-long into ashes:
kindred wondering about the end of time, then
the phoenix,
off in a certain distance,
like the rising Sun,
Vishnu sends a God-man, oneness Prophet,
Bahá'u'lláh, in a thrush of beauty,
"Peace! Peace!" and
a thousand thousand roses,
nightingales in spring, in spring.

III

Bahá, Exile, Prisoner, Rose,
Timeless Architect,
Tenth Avatar,
Reincarnation of Krishna,
Second Advent,
Prince of Peace, again,
the Mysterious in History,
Buddha of Universal Friendship,
unity-dancing is the way I have come to know Him.

IV

We re-create time
out of the fabric of timelessness;
He, she, I, we,
weave a garment of crimson
for the Prisoner.
Chains and torture,
forty years,
Isaiah circling around Him, Moses,

Muhammad,
His Odes in rivers
over the plain of Sharon.

V

The Prisoner
For Bahá'u'lláh, the Messenger of God

Prisoner, Exile,
Rose, Scion of Law,
Miracle of Reason –

Crimson Justice,
Eden's Phoenix, Man's Question,
Heaven's Answer –

VI

For our new vision, our regeneration,
with earth at spring,
its silo of winter ready,
I wake,
teeming prayers in my days,
like the ear of ritual,
devotion's incense,
bhakti, love,
I read the Bhagavad-Gita
of the Hindus
past midnight,
and rise at dawn

VII

My joy days
spent in the bosom of
the Song of Songs,
the Beatitudes,
the Epistles,
Isiah's roundness, His garden,
His temple of grandeur,
charging us to wideness.

The pearl.
The Crimson Ark of Bahá/escort in time/
out of time/
seasons in Jerusalem, New Jerusalem,
Ganges valley, Yangtse shadows, Nairobi nights,
Delhi days, Dharma days, Kyoto,
shadow and light, refraction of time,
unity-dance.

VIII

Thus, the commonwealth of man,
brotherhood and sisterhood,
this Tree of Life,
we are called
like earth and sky,
into the calamity of its reason,
like the remembrance of the moon,
Alláh'u'Abhá! Alláh'u'Abhá!

Rising Sun/aura of gladness/
tempest time wrung out of time/
Alleluia! Alleluia!
sundance/unity-dance/fling the cord of joy/high! high

IX

"You can kill me,
but you cannot stop the emancipation of
women!"
cries Táhirih, the feminist poet,
at her execution.

In the stillness of midnight,
the center of the universe is fire and light,
and a rose,
like that light upon light,
so often on the tongue of the son of Bahá'u'lláh,
'Abdu'l-Bahá, so strong, so tender.

X

I am immersed in the
sea of a New Jerusalem,
with those same rivers of Eden,
flowing through my mind.

I know stones by the river
and the tidal sensibility of an ocean.
I am coming to see
the green grass of Sharon
as gold, silver, treasure beyond treasure;

I gather the cypress to my mind
toward a gentle justice;
I fly over the hyacinth rainbow
I heal by;
a wanderer, sacred and worldly, like seas,
I search galaxies and become a star/
climb out of the mind into
things in themselves.

XI

The simple, the rich,
the poor, the Brahmin,
the underclass, the scholars,
all heard the new vision with praises,
I am won in the key of G to this wonder,
I am won in E flat,
I am won in F.

I am won in ragas,
lotus is my flower,
New Delhi is my far away, flyaway home.
I am won in Be-Bop
as Dizzy Gillespie, for fifty years,
plays the horn, so beautiful, so full of love,
happy-feet,
unity-dance,
a Bahá'í, this Dizzy.

XII

Roses, roses,
the Ode to Joy of Beethoven
in the time of Bahá,
declaring the oneness of the human race,
Dostoevsky, the same universal,
all on a Pegasus wind.

I carry my words
home to the farm,
home to the city,
far into and out of the mind of the maker,
across the careening sky.

XIII

I have wound my words around this Tree
and climb it like ivy;
I "redeem the time"
and remember, upon waking,
the depth and joy of music.
Roses are my chief concern,
art and religion embracing like fire and air,
a thousand years of peace,
time.

XIV

"The earth
is but one country
and mankind its citizens"
declares the Prophet.
The closing of these borders
whirls us
into the Global Village, a Union of States,
beyond blood-letting,
into a new meaning,
thrust by history's own fire.

Coming, coming,
Oslo, Prague, Beijing,
Moscow, New York,
Jerusalem,
new world, rising.

XV

We wring entropy out of time,
timelessness in time,
a centripetal force,
like the weaver's threads upon a spool,
a choreographed thing,
so divine, so awful,
"such courage, such passion,"
I remember Rilke saying we must
"hold to the difficult."

XVI

I am Jew,
I am Christian,
I am Moslem,
I am Buddhist,
I am Hindu,
I am Bahá'í,
then, in its oneness,
its unity-dance,
like the wings of the dove in motion,
I pray for peace,
and sweetly smell roses,
woodsmoke and honey in my own Shenandoah Valley,
hyacinths and anemones, across my years,
dying daily toward a good death,
the clay broken,
phoenix-rising.

XVII

The andante clarinet
on the recording in my room,
here, as I write,
remembering
the concert of Rubinstein
in the year of my graduation,
on stage,
within view of his precious
hands,
my sister and I,
breathless.

XVIII

The rainbow lingers;
we are ready, steadily working,
rising to a world
commonwealth,
our gaze steady on peace.

Language
redeems culture, it must;
and southern writers
renew us.

As Bahá'ís, then,
we are like reeds
out of a marsh, me,
s sprig of timothy,
bending to hear and breathe
the peace dream.

XIX

One day I went walking
in the tangled web of
lightning, rain and darkness
to year Joyce:

the Dead, the Dead, the Dead,
pitched in the motion of that seeing,
brewing, yeasting,
a time out of time,
suffering, making and remaking myself/
epiphanies following.

Living the Color Crimson

I

Jerusalem embraces America in my mind,
on the fifth year after a trip to Israel;

I see Arabs and Jews, Moslem, Christian, all
as the stars of one velvet sky,

heaven shared with Buddhist, Hindu and Confucian, equals;
the work of living peace, one vision,

Quetzalcoatl, side by side with Moses and Muhammad,
living religion as the Tao of all religions.

II

I like to think of being Bahá'í as
living as well as a gazelle runs,
being human in the image of eagles;

if dolphins are precious and beautiful,
so may be Bahá'ís, whether they bear the name
or not; I am thinking of ideal beings, like stars.

Something has fallen apart at the center of time
in our century; looking for an answer
has come to be as common as crisis;

I think of Bahá'í as the Easter
of a century of blood, as
the oneness of all humans, the epiphanies

of going to bed to the moon, and
waking to birdsong, as all-excelling as
being human well, as generous and bold
as the ocean itself.

III

Just over the hill
in my Shenandoah Valley town,
there are old orchards
where once I walked with my father.
In the mid-season
tumult of burgeoning apple trees,
we heard the bowing branches creak
with their fruitage.
That walk,
possibly taken more than once,
is etched in memory.

It is the peace
and the red breaths of history, mind in time,
my/our,
like New York, my father/World War II night flights/
like the Western Wall,
the Mount of Olives,
Mount Carmel,
peace, eternity, roses.

IV

To the witness of Eden,
there is little here in the way of blizzards,
but storm is
the reminder of the cruelty of history,
the heard lines of a well-planned battle, here, now,

as 180 nations gather in New York
to make plans for peace. No answers.

no way out,
only phoenix-fire burning.

V

The rest of doing
carries me,
like the piano man
who only wants to play his piano.

I live to be
and these poems are
my existence,

my heady aura
against the dark.

VI

I was
the only white man
in a gospel choir,
and the only white man
in a black jazz band.

My trumpet
still knows its way
to a sweet tone and
plays me to sleep
with a listening ear
to midnight.

I meditate with it, too,
and know myself better
because of its healing.
I chose a deli
where women, professionals,
students, working class,
black and white
come freely
to the music
of Gershwin's magic: jazz, classical,
and these Dylan tapes, others.

I remember Freddie Hubbard's first trumpet
was made
of a funnel and a garden hose
and keep to an old portable.

The shirt I wear today has the scripts
of six languages:
English, Russian, Hebrew, Japanese,

Greek and Arabic.
There is this race we must run.
Fritjof Kapra writes the Tao of Physics,
and my mind is bent
towards the fusion of two lovers,
science and religion,
embracing in the thoughts
of a physicist
outside the temples of Kyoto.

VII

Hope and despair intertwined
are the roses I live.
I learn of things as they are
by leaving them.

I see the host
and linger over it, sniff
the communion wine,
and move on.

Still,
I ache for liturgy,
for ritual,
for patterns
large enough to be a net
under days, days enough,
full enough to ride me high
into dying day.

VIII

On an odd day
I go to Quaker meeting or
discuss the Unitarian-Universalist Church
with my friend Paul.
There is so much of me that is wide and empty,
gaping,
agnostic like night.
Bahá'u'lláh speaks of God as the "Unknowable Essence."

I find this indefinite universe,
wide as time,
my own days as leonine as a century, at least
these thirty-odd years;
my meandering
as mortal as roses,
as incomplete as a single cherry table
without its room.
Feeling this wideness,

like the sea,
this bliss and ease of my untended garden,
I wind out my themes in song,
the blustering Irishman who is my father,
my mother, the composer of twenty children's musicals,
my brother, my sister, competent and kind,
these poems in the Shenandoah Valley like rain.

IX

I rehearse the tide of giving.

I look for this victory of peace,
against the background of the disappearing dead:
Dachau/Watts/Dr. King/Kennedy/Kennedy,

then charge myself
like a wave turning in upon itself
with the work here.

I will hide in the rock
and find my solace
in the ports of 180 nations.

X

On my knees;
university for the temple begins here.
Say your graces, and
do the fast at Yom Kippur,
for they are listening at the rabbi's table.

Still,
I remember
the single cherry blossom.

XI

I am as good as any amorous man
and cry over my Lord
with hard tears.

I seek only the resonant stone
in the light of light itself,

tying,
weaving,
the broken strands,

In my afternoon,
a global studies major,
working on his poems,

in my evening
a Bahá'í Chinese,
who remembers

his traditional family there,
blending Taoist, Confucian, Buddhist,
as the very epitome
of Chinese religion.
The next day,
coming into conversation
over pastries and coffee
with a Bahá'í who teaches at the Quaker
school nearby.

It is a coming into conversation.

Now
at the Hamburg Inn
in The Iowa Writers' Workshop,
a resolute heart,
next to the athlete,
remembering two years
driving a cab
for the senior citizens.
Nods to the retired farmer
at the table –
conversation opens up
into this complete embrace,
roses,
the fragrance of anemones,
living the color crimson.

From
From God's Whimsy
(1990)

———————————◆———————————

Latitudes of the Heart

In the latitudes the heart lives,
I see the relentless discovery
of the touchstones that remake us –

Through the brutal breakers
thrown at us, the human spirit,
regal, defiant, triumphant, reeling,

solves itself in some indeterminant code,
some lucid gamble on its own sovereign odds,
a high mystery that can only be called wonder.

In Sum

Below the ledge of earth,
there, in the holocaust room,
as death's starlings cackle,
I am confident of this, still –

that from our groaning bones,
hung with flesh or not,
comes a new light
that builds the city on the hill.

Breakfast

In the hotel in Jerusalem
we ate whole raw fish,
whole loaves of bread,
\whole eggs, hard-boiled,
and black olives, five or six different kinds –
each dish served in a basket,
twenty of them or so,
around the table, including
several kinds of bagels,
a separate bucket each
for jellies, butter and cream cheese –
I thought I would never finish
when an armed guard
flooded through the hotel lobby
out past a French import –
the morning had exploded
and the soldiers would hitchhike
from there to the front line in Lebanon –
\bending the meaning of justice
to a marching tune we never heard.

Numinous – Word, Lake and Power

Numinous, that word, speaks it –
no, the theologians have used it up –
yet, it meant light, luminous wondrous light –
the hard variety, that rigorous light –

I am thinking of the calloused hands
someone gets from handling a rare book collection –
the speaking it is to see a coal miner face on –
I am thinking of the man who goes to the diner, once,
does not stay as I have, that man, riding
a fine car, wonderful home, but heart enough to care
seeing that the working class needs a caring eye –
a hard diamond mind of compassion –
a regal levity at the right moment in negotiations –
a close reading of a talmudic tradition –
soundless feet at a Buddhist temple –
some real knowledge of Japanese tea ceremony –

I am thinking of priceless pearls passed by,
the merest wind of truth searched out,
hundreds of miles to swim in an honest lake –
this is a hint of what the theologians mean.

God's Whimsy

God's whimsy
     is to create Himself
thousands of millions of different ways,
       universes, making Himself,
          God's whimsy is to create man who creates –

I don't think God is past tear-jerkers,
         for what is it to send a young man
    into the lions –
       all at stake, life, principle, property,

God's eye is on the Roman in the crowd
        who cannot give up position, but
        breathes to himself that this is wrong –

God's whimsy could be
     the Blue Angel pilots and their jets,
     a peaceful peacetime sort of mission,
to fly endless flight in close formation,
     to twirl and twirl and twirl,
screaming by over crowds,
     neglecting their own safety,
emancipating the human need to
       soar –

     God's whimsy
likens itself to a cool-warm day in July
         sitting on enclosed balconies, overlooking a
    Martha's Vineyard scene,
       glasses of iced tea, tipped with lemon,
yearning for nothing at all,
       content with the absolute glory of no,
         delighted with yes,
       overcome with the grandeur of not quite,
          maybe dear, let's not today –

God's whimsy
must be like the canopied beds
        meant for wealthy couples,

for one night given to a poor lad
            and his girl,

            wonderful couple sort of things happening,
            a joyful noise is made,

morning breaks over our little vacation,
            God smiles

        God's whimsy
    is among the soldiers who at a truce,
come up to the demarcation line to chat –

        God's whimsy is there
            in the diner
    where the food is so cheap
    you can eat there every day,
and so good you want to –

        God's whimsy
    resides with the Persian sage
            who tells humorous stories
among America's wealthy and sophisticated,
            leaving religion aside –

God's whimsy is
      like the shade trees you always wanted,
and maybe had, trees under which nothing
          happened, over and over again.
      in such totally wonderful ways
          that no one could quite recall
      until years later, just how glorious it was

          O I am so tired
      being productive, caring about the news,
          I think I will stop wearing socks,
      I will forget to buy new shoes,
          I will leave my shoe laces untied a few days,

then, I will eat my fill of food and sleep awhile,
          and remember that I am not so handsome anymore,
and I have no real money of my own,
      but God's whimsy may be wishing me to live,
      God's whimsy may be in my bones, making days
          come and go.

From
Rhapsody
(1990)

1

Gentle me, my lamp, my luminous
touch, kindle, win me,
ambient angel –

show me your lean eyes,
ineluctable eyes, redolent eyes,
spin me through your universes

there in your limbs,
send me through your fusion self,
your Source, your beginnings –

2

lay me down on your handsome lay,
your weave of loveliness,
your generous rest –

gentle me down, and I will lift you
like a kite, my banner, my drink,
and I will be your prize –

each of us winding out our loftiness,
like the tuck of a jib,
like a thorough regard for breezes –

3

Blend this roaring heart
with your dark brilliance,
ebony on ivory in our eyes –

a readiness in the bowing stars,
a sharp longing warmed by morning,
you, my lute to play, I, your clavier,

or do you want a piano, forte and all,
largeness, room, spaces,
keys to spring a bit –

4

Maybe the genius of your singularity
lies in your fierce achievement,
your total loving –

so, we succeed as a work, if we do,
only because you surge with enthusiasm
for my doing, and I for yours,

winning the portals of the mind,
reading the old world as it passes away,
imagining new worlds to live. . . .

5

I sit here meaning you,
as if shape were invisible,
and could recline like mist –

my blue jeans or my khakis,
riding my hips like friends,
the way your memory conforms to me –

thinking that you are the emblem,
yes, the self I most admire, like a strand of light,
a perfect hieroglyph –

6

I sit toward the self,
like a wheel spinning toward
an ineluctable center –

nodding to the Source
that winds out its yearning,
singing you,

singing the real blue
where altitude is no longer a problem,
and we fire ourselves above the mountains –

7

We shirk nothing,
bending toward each task,
God inside so far

He is dark to us,
we, doing, being, becoming, all,
with the "suchness" of Zen –

each piece of grass an ideal,
watching the way an ant grows
on the temple steps –

8

So myself is yourself, and love,
we speak the crimson beyond the rainbow,
then, lean back for blueness,

leaving ourselves outside of it all,
finding ourselves in our wake,
like the "59th St. Bridge Song."

lamposts to coo at,
songs to sing all morning,
days to spend like good coin –

9

The regions of the self
seal our embrace, and we move
on toward community –

we kneel in the pine needles,
reading the moon like wildflowers,
needing, not needing –

wild, tended, untended,
crossed, patched, heeded, neglected,
out of bounds, on the mark.

From
Planet Dreams
(1991)

Shadow and Stone

I leaned into the shadows
the mind cast off –
losing whole histories of myself –
but found a larger God than before,
one who could break my fears
like dead branches and use them for fuel –
there in the darkest place of all,
the shattered soul,
I discovered the quirky God
who could laugh with me,
realize a dream larger than my hopes
and put it all away
in the hip pocket, like a stone,
to polish and dream on again.

Floating on the Edge

I sat there at the edge,
the edge where you lean over
and look at the roots of the world
from sixty-thousand feet –
and I locked onto the idea that
God could be found by floating –
I proved this out
over a span of forty-five hundred test flights –
which just goes to show
that a good hypothesis
can overcome a shortage
in laboratory equipment
and university budget –
despite the odds that
experimenters can explode
on atmospheric re-entry
wearing only blue jeans and a flannel shirt.

Transportation

I sit here, 6 A.M.,
on a Saturday, riding
through the grey mist,
still riding foolish,
in the counter seat at the diner –
driving the car to Maine,
riding the train to New York, to Boston –
riding in the plane to Israel
where soldiers are still
hitchhiking in civilian Volvos
to the front of Lebanon – with M-16s –
I am still in school, listening
to a lecture, here in the chair –
I am riding the lesson back home
from college to research migrant labor
and I am driving to Washington
to work for a Nader group –
I am on the subway to work –
I am reading the morning *Post* in my chair
and I am rolling in your arms.

Colorado Spruce

I wanted to be a willow
I've wanted to be a pine
I love the dear dogwood and
I know a red maple nearby –

But I think today,
I'll be the Colorado Spruce
my father has planted
in the back of our house –
a lofty blue-green –
settling in for fifty years of growth,
by the shade of the mountains,
the crystal accompaniment of
the river's song.

Night, Night Listen Well

Night, night listen
to these troubles, night –
you can hide them
in your disappearing self –
you know a black hole
to steal away to –

all the meter is gone,
all the stanzas reel off
into space, the couplets
sting like overgrown children –
I am an iamb to myself –
neither more nor less,
simply being in time –
mortal, refused, denied, found,
and molded to some hand of unsure destiny –
take these away night,
take these meanings
off the wall and
make them day.

Going to the Universe

"I'll be going
to the universe today, dear,
don't wait up.
Naturally, I'll call
when I find a hotel,
Be sure to water the plants
and don't forget
to change the sun.
I may be gone for awhile,
Do give my best
to geology,
and remember me to physics –
it's been so long,
I miss you already,
my dear, dear planet, so long –
your moon loves you –
bye-bye. . . ."

From
Songs for the Phoenix
Selected Poems (1984–1994)
(Selections VII–X)

Midnight

Final things of the day –
letting go of a breath
as morning takes in –

outside – midnight –
pins of light all around me –
city lights – planes – stars – planets –

I reach into my pocket,
tossing a quarter into the dark – spinning sparks –
it realizes itself in my hand –

I stand there like a rod –
planted in the ground – a scepter –
a column in my family's building –

the night is food to me –
the air is a beverage –
bricks of the house are pylons for heaven –

I touch each artifact
in this present history – a blade of grass –
a sprig of mint – the wind is tipped with lemon.

Shades of Violet

Violets, violets,
        I am seeing the world,
region by region, in shades of violet –

my Shenandoah summer
        lies violet and clipped,
like a fair vase in itself –

New England, cusp and apex,
        from Danbury to Kennebunk,
laughs awhile in these colors –

something Scandinavian,
        something sleepy and African,
I am thinking of gentle passions in violet.

A Poem of Friendship

I would see it this way –
that of all things gold,
and all things sterling,

a higher sort of friendship,
immersed in love or not,
this stands apart in mystery –

like the reasons of day,
or the logic of singing,
the fact of a friend, this is enough

to sway storms or seasons,
to settle continents
into a single town.

Autumn Luck

A feisty wind
with the autumn luck
to twirl a bit –

a leaf engages
in resolute drift,
conversing with the definite air –

The God of all seasons
tips the moment
with light rippling on burnt orange.

The Origin of Singing

The whole heuristic hum
there, in the absolute trees,
lives like a perfect song,
in the resolute heart –

a certain reeling joy
careens off the sky,
creating a way to see
out of the rimmed hearing
where God sings the hours,
we listen to the song,
forming a tradition of singing,
out of the most resonant clay.

A New Rising

Advent, 1991

The spent husks
fall into a pile,

hugging the earth,
one by one, layered
like ruins –

on this rug of memory
a new hope is prayed,
a new hinge is levered –

the old ache died well –
let a new thing rise, a royal falcon,
a bird of high resolve –

a new rising is shouldered.

Oneness Wings

The whole inexorable flex
of the unfolding world Tao
  triumphs on oneness wings –

the Bahá'í-Buddhist-Christian
swim resolves into a kind of delta
where river-life meshes into one ocean –

I am thinking of a place
where Buddhist monks and
Bahá'í teachers and agnostic seekers

can work with simple, sufficient tools
to build a cabin in the woods –
a place to face the big empty.

A Tincture of the Absolute

A tincture of the absolute
would be enough – a suggestion,

a limned, crescent moon scoring the dark a bit –
a fold here, a tuck there in the canvas of night

showing the way light bends –
the spectrum is not just one color –

nor is the way home single – God may be kaleidoscopic.

Letter to God

For Roger White

Your High Majesty, Sire
O Consequential, O Dire Abundance –
O Impelling Giver –

Your servant Roger,
Roger White, poet, friend,
wit, gallant, buckler

to the Bahá'í Revelation –
this Roger, the Roger of the *bon mot*,
Roger of the well-crafted poem,

he is no longer among us –
be well settled with him, Sire,
content yourself with his deeds –

confess him among your people –
make his name bright in paradise then,
conquer unhappiness with him,
make his radiance unending.

A Surmise of Elegance

As we approached the Brown Palace Hotel,
a surmise of elegance
gained on my flying time to Denver –

the doorman held the solid brass door –
the bellman met me inside –
high tea was waiting –

a string quartet played Mozart –
momentarily, four-star dining within –
upstairs, the maid was turning down your bed.

The Edge of the Galaxy

I sing you
a certitude of earth,
in its plenitude –

its full-throated
well-singing floating
around the edge

of the galaxy, beyond
the vibrant center,
here, where the swell

of darksome space
ranges out in leagues,
fathoms to swim –

beyond, beyond,
our yearning missives
to the deep unknown, serve notice
that we are here, and we are waiting.

The Environmentalist

For my brother

You are a his and hers blues specialist
you have expertise in the Way of Zen –

you have historic meetings with your mind in the restaurant
you travel to a New England town meeting on the ocean's
coast-

you talk on the phone like a dolphin
you ride the train into the future, your own porter –

you are beautiful, your Irish folk songs are beautiful
you like high tech, low tech, inside-outside days –

you watch an Andes year go by and find your find
you/you/ – you live like cajuns, like gypsies –

you dance the dance on the common ground,
you fly to the West Coast or Kyoto, watching the wing.

Outlandish Gratitude

What cold lock on things
melts a bit with whimsy
what spent heart
heals a bit with a dance—

the crucial questions
lean on laughter
solemnity lives toward
the logic of its own release—

God releases us, I think,
from the chains of our making
when our gift explodes
with outlandish, roaring gratitude.

Meditation

How to sum up, here,
Sunday morning, mid-winter –
then, isn't the divine an ache –
 isn't it a way home –

would a single sparrow be
enough? Is a meditation
on a single leaf about right?
Are we already there?

A Friend's Farm

Sharon and Arthur order a cord
of mixed soft and hard wood,
mostly hard for a slow burn,
and we lean into the cold evening
like sparrows.

Sharon has some new herb remedies
and the moon is nearly full.
We chart a course for the world
or baby Duncan,
breath following breath,

Eden on our brows
like incense
or the cost of our food –

forty-five cents each
for a pack of
cucumber, tomato or lettuce seeds last spring,
lights in the coop for a year,
enough stone and corn
to feed the chickens
long enough to lay a dozen eggs,
potatoes from potatoes from potatoes.

Canaveral Couplets

A miracle of light mounted the sky
with its jets, a propulsion liberty

wrought out of steel. A cathedral of fire,
this angel of warning, this limb of the whole of man,

climbed the millenia of history.
It caromed into and beyond

gravity's grasp, and sound broke.
A complex of mind and metal

bent its course toward the purple planets.
A myriad constancies came into play

as instruments made emptiness redolent
and the merest bit of darkness became

the discovery of habitable space.

Nightingales and Roses

Ridván, April 21—May 2

Ridván, paradise, home –
in spring, situate on an island,
prisoner, house arrest, nonetheless,
then Baha'u'llah declared
His Liberations, His new freedom –

in that place, slavery broke
its insolvent back – equality
made magnum progress – roses,
nightingales and joy broke forth
amid a roaring justice –

this was a particular grace
of a Spirit-King – this, the giant
munificence of a High Prophet –
to free women in a single breath –
to watch it unfold is history.

An Evening Performance

At the evening performance,
the trumpet player, first chair,

settled his embouchure with a glass
of water, then a handkerchief,

glanced briefly at the audience,
the house full, dressed to the nines,

leaving no doubt to the rising
portals of sound as the brass quintet

left the earth with Fanfare for the Common
Man,
Copland etching phrases of eternal yes,

across the evening and across the century,
making the word clarion brand new.

Diner Days

Endless refills
on 6 A.M. cups of coffee
for the ham-fisted men at the counter –

waitresses straight out of the depression
with names like Frankie, Thelma Lou
Doris and Dee Dee –

sausage gravy, scrapple,
home fries, and morning papers –
businessmen running business from a booth.

Gabriel Has Taken Wing

For Dizzy Gillespie

Gabriel has taken wing –
a horn so plentiful and full,
full of the pyrotechnics of love –

an ecstatic re-invention of Eden –
fundamentals turned to spirals
of sound trumpeting joy –

today, center stage is deep
with an empty space as large
as history will allow –

Be-Bop is left without currents of memory –
the horizon of jazz is dimmed –
America, the world, and the Bahá'ís

wait to hear heaven blow –
we have stardust to reckon with –
Louis has company now –
Dizzy has gone to join the saints.

From
The Holy Passions
(1998)

The Holy Passions

Give me the holy passions –
the high ambitions of the Rose –
for Ireland loves a martyr
and wide is the needle's eye in mercy –

everything says either yes or no
to Eden, to Gilead, to Jerusalem
and this is the wide embrace –

I am concerned with the music,
the music of epiphanies all year long,
and Easters in the heart of the average person –

it is hot cries in the desert,
followed by sweet-pouring water,
wrought out of God's own giving –
a giving so complete, so total,

that it is won just by going,
just by believing that much
in the endless pageant of human need.

Decibels

I remember the decibels
     of unspent, yet targeted
         nuclear warheads,
     driving riveted terror
         into the back of my head
    since the age of eight,
         tension mounting on tension,

like you maybe,
    the Cuban Missile Crisis,
    splitting like a spear
  into my hearing,
         spared, lucky to be alive,
    trajectory over thirty years,
into the confessional of the street
    where enough is enough –
not wanting it, but "diving
    into the wreck" –
how your feelings pack in,
    then, pack in again, then snap –
      how nuclear stress
         took half your time
         just facing it.

Report from the Edge

Reporting from the edge,
where the edge is the usual space,
and the air either cuts like ice,
or heals you, it's so tropical –

the losses weigh in like shipwrecks,
the orchestras are cities, and
the women are Hindu goddesses –
the boddhisatvas hang out in the Village –

here, world peace is guaranteed
by jazz bands – the police are hip –
and the hipsters swing just by
forgetting to show up for war –

this is a jazz-classical swing –
it is an ethical electricity –
this is a way to do the road
just by traveling in the mind.

Divine Logic: The Bahá'í World Centre

With the first line of reasoning
             as a row of cypress,
a strategy of roses and anemones follows –

             a logic of terraces,
       and world class marble,
             plus the argumentation of palm trees –

neo-classical and Eastern architecture
             combine like edicts,
       over a rational proof of ivy –

       faith is won on brick walkways,
       among hedges and hyacinths,
and heavy wood-carved doors at the Shrines –

       an inescapable conclusion
       rendered in your own tears,
             a judgment made of rose-water, a
light touch on the shoulder,
             an Israeli sunset forged in burnt orange.

Haikus for Earth

1

As Native Americans know,
     "we are all related" –
a root system is one thing –

2

A lapidary turns
     the earth like a stone –
each country a jewel –

3

There is a great heart
     in a sea-bird –
a survivor's heart, and wings –

4

A red maple standing
     full and free –
a most perfect zephyr –

5

I live a solar day –
     active and passive,
between wind and sun.

A Clearing

I wash my reluctance
in itself, thinking of the wisdom
of leaving well enough alone –

it is winter now, so
whenever it is winter within,
I give myself right of way

to cover my obligations,
then, take a proper retreat to fireplace,
to friends, to hearth, to self –

if the thicket around me,
and in my mind, fails to fall clear,
I give myself rights

to this soul of mine,
to cut a clearing I can call my own,
a place to stand.

Christmas Vespers

In the early cold nights
     of the season, I think of hot cider
        by the wood stove,
tree-lined streets with candles in the windows,
     a community chorus singing the Messiah,
        a brass choir, a soloist on Christmas Eve –

then, I am in the early days of this new-old
     religion, and I am a Druid minstrel,
    tuning his heart to hear the music
      of the baby Jesus –

then, I am a Byzantine priest, touring
     an elaborate passageway
to the library, to find an early scroll –

or, am I myself, during the war of 1982,
     buying gum from a Palestinian child
outside the church of Bethlehem –

or, am I in the heartwood of my life,
     watching the luminaries on the street,
   in my neighborhood, waiting for the next pass
     of the winter sleigh and horses,
       ivy draped along the side.

Harbors of the Heart

In the harbors of the heart,
there is an inlet I'm keeping
as a vessel for my beloved –

it is a well-kept cove, off
the usual sea-ways – there,
her silences will be musical,

her off-hand remarks will
resonate like chimed bells –
my hopes settle in those moorings

.

Jo-Jo's Song

Jo-Jo works at the burger
joint – her skin is dark
as chestnuts – hair as black
as a lake at midnight –

Jo-Jo is genuine as good
blues, as real as railroads –
there is no forgetting
the blood is red, no matter

what your skin color – Jo-Jo
works late and early –
minimum wage and she'll take
your order with a smile.

Changeless Light Upon Light

In all the changeless light
    in the nature of light,
of all the billion milliseconds
    in a spectrometer,

there is something undeniable
    in the generous light
that pours across the canvas
    each day – the thing itself –

there is something so utterly good –
    so unspeakably given –
daylight – sheer radical daylight –
    I am not through noticing –

No, I am not through noticing yet –
    how shafts of light,
hundreds of them – in one town alone –
    makes window poems –

the genius of the Deity in sunbursts
    around every cloud –
what high-kicking fun for God to shed
    light, upon light, upon light.

Bahá'í Cool

for Billy Roberts

The thing is, this guy
waltzes into a new airport
every week or two –

gold card and $200 –
registers in the medium up
hotels – jazz band,

pool, and you can
take your mother –
swings when he walks –

knows Zen and can handle
the Wall Street Journal –
then this magician

talks like family
to four hundred faces –
they're in tears, and

he's ready for the monogrammed
kerchief himself – steps out
late with a needful one –

Bahá'í cool – got his own –
uptown – downtown.

Outrageous Sweet Planet

Burritos for breakfast, a call
to Geneva by noon, an Indian
restaurant tonight, American rock
to drive me through to jazz –

my friend Howard is just back
from development work in Chile –
my brother John, a working meeting
in Nairobi, then Rio for the Earth Summit –

Australian Aboriginal dancers here
in my colonial Virginia – Native
American dancers, too – Doc Holladay
on African flute – one million people

on satellite hook-up to the Bahá'í
World Congress in New York, then,
an old tune from Nat King Cole –
I sing you, outrageous sweet planet.

The Church of the Big Blue Dome

I think the church of the big blue
       dome may be enough –
the sky has its own cavernous music –

but, then, a friend and I have invented
       the Zen Baptist Church –
no membership, no meetings, just send money –

He paints Chinese water colors, and I
       make coffee money on poetry –
no wealth like good international java –

I will take the house of leaves that a tree is –
       I will suffice myself with this –
the sling of mercy that is the Great Tao.

Proud Sunset

As the last light of evening
tumbles down the sky,
a proud sunset wrought
from burnt-orange flares out –
the August auburn clouds
stack up in cumulus layers
almost the geologic strata –

I think of the Outer Banks
or a place off Cape Cod
where I might go if I were
not scheduled into a cage –

by ten, a limned purple
tips evening with its clean passion –

then, the moon rises off
the baseline of the trees –
rolls across the blue-black sky
and spends its luminosity
on the earth like a mother –

I take a breath of cool
out the door into the fields,
reading the shadowed, tired
outposts to the dark.

The Question of a Mama

Whole leagues of yearning
      on the question of a mama –
How do you frame it?
a mama – who means stitches in your sleeve,
      or your ego – who is a piece of your history –
who stands for being happy –
      despite yourself –

      a mama – who counts what you're feeling –
      who rests on your laurels –
      who tucked in night's child –

mama – who gave reasons to the dark –
      who hugged you and your world,
         then, gave them away –
you have both still,
      because she gave so well.

World Religion

Tomorrow you drive
down Rt. 29 near Charlottesville,
to the Hindu temple,
    where they quote Bahá'í
    and honor all other religions –

but, today you have ambled
out Rt. 50 to the Buddhist center,
a monastery, where each monk
    retreats to his own
    hermitage in the woods –

your Catholic friend meditates
according to an Indian tradition –
your father reads the Way of Zen –
Jain friends attend the Bahá'í
    meeting, the alternative priest
    suggests lunch, where he talks
    about helping on the West Bank.

Farvashi, Inner Light

The Zoroastrians call it
　　　farvashi –
the Quakers call it inner
　　　light –
The Hindus have it spark
　　　of the eternal –
it is about ambient Tao,
　　　within –

it is about something in
　　　the chest –
it is the shape of mind –
　　　heart –
opening out onto the
　　　world,
an envelope holding
　　　the higher self,

tucking up here and there,
　　　relying on lotus,
on a sense of what might be,
　　　on prayer, on the numinous.

Song for Jerusalem

On the hill above
the Kidron Valley
outside Jerusalem,
but within sight
of the Old City,
  you see olive trees
  two thousand years old

within the city limits
there is rainfall
of twenty-two inches
per annum – across
the road, the Judean
  desert exits buildings
  and conflict at one inch per year –

there is no leaving
this space, and after that
laughter and tears,
each, are arrivals –
sunscape and limestone
buildings, spare and simple,
  the Arab market,
  threaded by the way of the cross.

Journey Poem

In Jerusalem, the Old City
     invites the wanderer
into four Quarters, Jewish,
     Arab, Christian and Armenian –

most building is in limestone –
     we go to the Arab Quarter
for dinner, fifteen courses,
     olives in five kinds,

several salads, bread, hummus,
     baklava, pitas, others –
you stay at the hotel where
     troops rush out to the front –

Bethlehem, the white church near
     the traditional site
of Christ's birth – a Palestinian
     child selling bubble gum –

the Sea of Galilee, temperate
     and calm, below the Golan
Heights – you miss Nazareth,
     because of an ammunition

explosion at the kibbutz
     in Tiberias, the shock of it,
explosions nearby, an hour and a half
     in the bomb shelter.

A Gathering in the Backyard

A federation of trees,
mostly, a consortium of evergreen,
gather in the backyard –

Norway spruce, white pine,
and juniper, mix with a couple
of red and silver maple –

I have such a mirror
to look in, with these trees –
a visit with the other side almost –

at the bottom of our hill,
a Colorado spruce, lifting
its blue-green yearning to forever.

The Red Maple

A tree, a red maple,
stands outside my window
and caresses the night –

it is burgeoning with leaves,
each a deep russet shade of red –
we have let it grow

so that it branches,
like huge hands, hunker down
low to the ground with heft –

I lay down the weight
of my day's doing late at night,
and listen to the leaves whisper,
swish, and bob, in the cool air.

Vortex

Martyrdom of the Bab, July 9

At the pinnacle of giving
beyond giving, the Bab
rides high noon into the vortex –

this young man, merchant,
spirit-genius, breaks open
a millennium at the deep end

of seven hundred and fifty rifles –
history implodes one hot day
in Tabriz – remember that day,

and learn the inside of giving double –
learn ultimate things in the fleck of a second –
weep at what it takes to win time's arc.

How Articulate, The Dead

How many times must they
desecrate the sacred –

a soulless cultural center
slated to go up where

Tehran's Bahá'í Cemetery
held thousands of bodies,

heroes and martyrs, in memory –
the government has asked

the contractor to work three shifts,
disinterring the dead –

how many profanations
to wake the living – how much,

the bodies, lifted up, will
proclaim their Lord again –

how articulate, the dead –
how mute, this culture of death.

The Dharma Café

Jack Kerouac blew into town
from the other world,

driving a cloud of mist,
sat down for a cup of Colombia Supremo,

then, quoted from the Tao Te Ching,
something about the Wu-Wei –

he looked great,
for a dead man –

started talking about the old days,
Ferlinghetti, Ginsberg, San Francisco, the road –

I asked him about the other side –
 he called it "The Dharma Cafe"

said he never felt better,
kind of like being a few centuries young –

at the end of his cup, he heard in his mind
that Mingus was about to play, over there,

so he got up in his blue denim,
then sauntered through the wall.

Crimson Elegy

The continents are adrift –
The English Channel has run dry –
The wind is running backward –
Bahá'u'lláh is dead –

The cups are full with emptiness –
The hills are flat in their places –
The merchants are closing up, no point,
Bahá'u'lláh is dead –

Dry off the taps – Sleep or not,
There is no sleeping – Forget yourself,
Remember where you came from,
Bahá, the King, is dead.

After Long Effort

At the end of long effort,
    there rises a gleam
on the rim of the world –
    this cream, this effusion,
signals the soul "well done" –
    what is accomplished thus
stands in the heart like a flag –
    a long, arduous road,
whether inner or outer, is much
    like winning the prize –
but so often, we must win it
    again and again, until
at last, we walk on summits,
    and make each day
a banner – then, when falling is
    falling and humans are mortal,
we fall not so far, nor does losing
    seem so much like losing –
at the end of long effort, deeds
    are in us, and our bones
know the keys and doors of doing –
    out heart, then, knows a high place,
and we go there, and we take a seat
    among the worthy and the strong,
keeping salutations for the meek, for winter,
    for God, for grace, for charm, and love, at last.

Dust of the Heart

"Bring thyself to account each day."

—*Bahá'u'lláh*

In the primary dust
of the human heart,
where we learn of ourselves,
break ourselves and become,
I go in each day to do
a bit of cleaning –
do not mistake me –
I love the dust – it is
quietly intrinsic to my wondering –
it is how I know I have been
to my wheels and churning –
nonetheless, I go in
and sweep up – I take account –
I bring myself to my knees
to taste my fool self –

then, out of the remains,
I claim my victories, and I sing tomorrow.

Shenandoah Song

On the waters
of the gently swaying
Shenandoah, I see
the men fishing, stretched
like a net, each with an eyelet,
across a dam, as the river
runs through their feet –
this is an old river,
and God has given it trees,
floodplain and a name –
it is my brother,
it is sister-life,
through the Valley,
each current, a strand,
in its tapestry.

Dreaming a New Velocity

I am dreaming a new velocity
    for the spring of things –
how the stones sing double-time –

how the plant spirits are leaping –
    how the trees reel –
a thinking that is a double-dream –
    how the ageless heart
of the improbable opens up now –

how the whole human prospect
    depends on the earth
and its gorgeous-hearted spin.

Dreaming It New

A tanka

I am dreaming an economy
  made of fibres of light –
    "light upon light" –

a world where law
bends into the fabric of being.

Dancing at the New World Café

I wander over to the pita bread,
and tuck up some tabouleh,
think some new Eden thought,
 and pray with my feet –

I am lost without baklava,
and remember myself with falafel –
the band is playing with sitar,
 digeridoo, and Nigerian drums –

O Dios, chant with us,
make us your music, unfurl
your flags with us, for a new world,
banners of peace and joy –

console us with your magnitudes,
forge in us a new honor,
suffice us with your altitudes,
dance with us at the new world café.

Night's Celebration

In the sweet blue-black,
I ride the night sky,
holding the wheel between
a finger and a thumb –

the road rolls out like a stream,
a runway for God's afterthoughts –
the tires turn with steam
toward the horizon they consume –

the sky is a rich pile of velvet,
you play some rock'n'roll,
and watch the city lights dance –
you make time stand still,

there where forever is almost
on your tongue – your body
leans into the speed and the hills
rejoice in night's celebration.

December Evening

On a December evening,
a folk guitar player
almost chants a song
about the holiday season –

she is surrounded by instruments,
a digeridoo, an Aboriginal wind,
a Native American drum,
a Nigerian drum, a sitar –

during the course of the night,
she will pluck, pound, blow,
as she celebrates the Solstice,
Hanukkah, Christmas, Kwanza,

even the Chinese New Year,
each in uttered succession like lights.

The Master Is Gone Tonight

Ascension of 'Abdu'l-Bahá

Ah, 'Abdu'l-Bahá, there should
           have been mansions,
dancers, musicians at court,

there should have been untold
           soirées, visitors
from the continent, endless

contentments – but there in
           prison, house arrest,
there were difficulties amid

difficulties – you left amid
           trouble, while you
slayed the troubles of others –

breakfast was bread and cheese –
           even night was not
free of trips to help the poor –

your city weeps tonight as do
           the friends – give out
the call, the Master is gone tonight.

This River, This Thunder

This river, this thunder,
this roaring of the Deity,
to break open the new era
with thunderbolts of transformation –

so horrifically, to unsuit
the world to war – so
drastically, to drive us
to our destined oneness –

with all impelling power,
with implicit glory, the hand
of history has unfastened
the old, and wrought a new justice –

rise up, scions of the hour –
drive on, locomotive of time.

Dancing at the Thorazine Hotel

At the thorazine hotel,
I danced with her a few minutes –
the staff considered
any co-ed contact dangerous –

we savoured every second –
her rounded frame sloped
sweetly into my hands –
the head nurse glanced hard

at me as she passed by –
but did nothing – I was within
a week of discharge – time
unravels twenty-year marriages –

nothing will touch those
perfect minutes in the rec.
room, dancing to the only
record in the place.

We

We sing of one free planet –
we hum a new thing, open –
we read the news in blue –
we form the future out of our clay –

we are the heirs of a new world –
we befriend the earth –
we celebrate all peoples, all hues –
we remember war no more –

we are dolphins, whales, and gazelles –
we whirl into the new being –
we toss trouble over into joy –
we forge a new bliss –

we are coming into sweet valleys –
we take a road to high places –
we sing a tune of all that is –
we ride a train to the new Eden.

Joy-Day
The Birth of Baháʼuʼlláh

This joy-day, this cusp
of core promise, nearly
exploding with light and fruitage –

here, the "son is given" –
here, the "child is born" –
and the government, we are building –

this consonant day sings out
with choirs across the centuries –
 it is high honor to attend Him –

this child – this luminary – this torch –
oblige yourself to your joy –
serve the Eden train in bliss.

Christmas Eve Canticle

In the deepening dark
of Christmas Eve,
as star-shine scintillates
on the nestling snow,

I give you hearty hail
for the season, that things
may not grow severe with you,
that the further reaches

of your dreams may draw
into focus, and blossom
that each year may spark
a new delight with living,

here, in the heart of things –
here, where the mantle shimmers with light.

Charleston Vignette

At one long sweet remove
from obligation, I taste

a piece of sky, a glimpse
of palm tree, swishing

the air – a hint of azalea,
the mention of quince,

and ocean air through the
yard – Old Charleston

awaits like a beacon
where the light of double-

porches will scan the sea-
breeze, homes on the Battery

will impress, and the South
will wear her best clothes

to the sound of jazz lofted
like laurels from the Market.

Shenandoah Vignette

Down Rt. 50 by the banks
of the Shenandoah, I would
paint a canvas of those waters,

a by-way from the trees
by the river, up toward
the monastery, where Buddhist

and Catholic monks learn
to agree on the Tao
from different windows –

further than I go today,
a canoe cuts these currents,
and leaves a wake at sunset.

She

She is the artist of her own becoming, the
    friend of her own needs –
She is a river among all rivers, unfolding –
    the mapmaker of her own mind –
She is giver, protector, provider, source –
    a confidant and doer –
She is sufficient to her solitude, yet,
    solidarity for her is tribal –
She is aware of the living flow,
    yet able to say a solid no –
She is a buttress, bulwark, partner,
    yet, ample to herself –
She weaves her tapestry of being
    on a loom of her making –
She relates, she executes, she is kind –
    yet, she knows her way to toughness –
She knows the by-ways of the heart –
    and the landscapes of the mind —
She is ambassador to her world –
    the royalty of her own heart.

To Honor a Titan

for Bahá'u'lláh

Bahá as the Great Ardor
describes an arc between
the darkness of the pit,

borne for His beliefs,
and a brilliant spiritual accuracy –
when He speaks, the light and thunder

of a Titan split the horizon,
with the capacity to mediate roses –
if His shoulder is mighty, then

His touch is elusive, suggestive,
gently complete – it is an honor to bear
His banner, a joy to have found the dance.

Skyscape

In the event no one noticed,
the sky itself was an event
tonight – with tufted clouds
of perfect white, russet, and auburn –
and you can see the light show

from your backyard – above
the trees, the skyscape climbs
into stratospheric expression
of the first Artist – He tosses
His paints across the sky every night.

Song of Unity

I sing a lucid unity tonight –
a wider sense of community –
a federation of leaves in each tree –

the unity of Native Americans
since the time of Pontiac –
the oneness of water from Lake Michigan

to the Mediterranean –
the quiet unity in a work of art –
body and spirit like sisters –

the single vision of a glass
of sparkling water, edged in cherry –
the walking mall with its historic buildings,

or a team of baseball players,
tucked like bats into a line-up –
a player's game, unified and fluid –

the life of Christ headed toward
that single, ineluctable moment on the cross –
time – varied currents, one absolute river –

sweet variousness in the heart
of a city park, many hues, one song –
many flavors, one people, at the street festival.

A Light from Persia

The Declaration of the Báb, May 23rd

A light from Persia
penetrates the closing dark –
there are decibels

in the quiet steps
of a young scholar on his quest –
when Mullá Husayn finds

the Promised One,
the Báb unfolds the text
with definite grace,

an explosion of white heat –
dark hopes implode there –
the new light is joined

to its task – concentric
circles of spirit-thunder follow –
the New Era is conceived.

Local Pottery and a Jamaican Band

Buddhists use the term
"suchness" – there is a coffee house
here in town where they sell

cappucino, café latte,
Indonesian dark, Guatemalan,
Viennese and Colombian –

I am sitting on the old town
mall, elsewhere, sipping a non-alcoholic
brew, at the café tables outside –

the Handworks Gallery
sells handmade rugs, tapestries,
and local pottery –

later today, I will talk
to my aunt, who practices Reiki,
a form of Japanese healing –

later this week, Jamaican
steel drums on the walking mall, in front
of the Old Courthouse.

Photo of 'Abdu'l-Bahá on facing page by Elise Pumpelly Cabot

The Smile, The Portrait

The Master knows you –
he knows the whole of you –
but, he will wait until
life turns you to Him –

the picture in Dublin, N.H.
shows Him at rest, hands
those hands, turned up
in His lap – never pointing –

the smile permits
even as it forgives – He is
through with judgement only –
He waits for you to wake –

It is also as if
He enjoys your mundane
desires, your fancies,
your heart all a jumble –

then, somehow, life itself
breaks into your forgetfulness –
the Master will be there,
there, to pick up the pieces.

Elegy for the King, Bahá

The Deity has passed into His deepness.
His roaring and His justice drive no more.
Bahá has gone into the earth and the ground
broods down with the bones. The God-Man
broke the earth and He did not break.

The rolling Pen is still. Triumph in the
dark, then, let nihil thunder with light.
Bahá is no vain thing, but king
enough to mount the ramparts of peace.
Be still, then, earth, for thy King is still.

Go no more idle and foolish – break
the silent sorrow-chords on your brows.

Architecture for a New World

We are in a tectonic space,
where continents and decades
slip and surge with massive drift –

but we do not have time
for eons to ease in and out
of view, indifferent to whole peoples –

we must learn to wrestle
with the architectonics of the future,
even as we ride the world-wave

of the present – the architecture
of a new world would account for slippage,
and mark well a certain tolerance

in the brick and mortar – it would
cohere with intrinsic solidity –
we urge up toward oneness like incense
in a house that is a prayer to build.

Peace Dream

This dream is about a Sunday
       morning in the future
when sweet, ineluctable things

occur, as if religion were meant
       for peace – it is about
the culture, church by church,

synagogue by synagogue, gathering
       as one congregation –
this is about the saffron robes

of Buddhist monks, sitting side by
       side with Catholic
Muslim, Hindu, in a Christian church –

all manner of combinations otherwise –
       until everybody is
having such a grand time it doesn't matter –

we all then want to be together so much
       we meet at the lunch
counters mid-week, and intermarry –

joy-days like those are the roses
       of history –
one congregation of the whole.

Sentinels of Peace

Wolfeboro, N.H.

Deeper than quiet,
the hum of the New Hampshire
lake town
envelops and releases the heart

into the chambers of its own freedom –
the trees on the drive
stand like sentinels of peace –
the voices of the city still,

and the union of pine
forms a federation of hillsides,
magistrates overseeing
the paddlewheel on the lake –

the boats churn the water,
the loons chant the night open,
and late night skyscape
explodes with a congress of stars.

The Roots of Jazz

From the shores
of West Africa, where the drums
and flutes would play

as message systems,
as celebrations of the coming
and going of day –

then, to the slave ships,
where most of the inmates died,
yet sang in work-rhythm –

to be sold at auction,
then, blending the sound of Africa
with the hymn tunes –

Underground Railroad,
spirituals as chants to set the people
free, exit to music –

then, the blues urging up
out of the belly of the South –
Satchmo and Duke, defining

the new sound – Count Basie joy –
Dizzy and Bird, then Coltrane, making,
praying up a revolution, Kind of Blue, with Miles –
up the century, like one long love train to Eden.

Death and the Robe of Heaven

Death is a carriage
that comes to draw us up
to the Great Lover –

when time ceases and
timelessness begins,
we fall into the cupped hand

of immortality and whirl
into the starlit world
of being beyond being –

we leave off the garment
of nature, and take on
heaven's robe, to wear

through cycles and ages,
untouched by these sorrows,
or this passing stage.

A Lover's Song

So may the Sun and Moon
be with us, and the Changeless One –
may our walk together
be until the end of darkness,
and the end of light –

may our words be like pearls,
and our days be like moonbeams –
may the rivers we live
be waters of much laughing –
in our time, may the world

forget to go to war –
may our song be the world's song –
may our embraces deepen and ripen,
until at last, we are taken
into the deepness of God forever.

Anthems for Earth
(2002)

From the bo trees of India
        to the cypress of Israel,
to a bagel at the interfaith
        conference here in Virginia,

I lean into the necessary dreams
        of peace, despite the dark –
a sand painting from the Navajo,
        a chat with a Sufi,
as a Buddhist monk drifts by.

———————— ◆ ————————

I sip a Costa Rican coffee
        and compare notes
with a Unitarian minister.
        On the wall hangs

a quotation from Black Elk.
        Outside Canada geese
gather their energies
        for the long flight south.
A Bahá'í artist – A Hindu Swami.

Horace Mann, the educator
       wrote, "Be ashamed
to die until you have won
       some victory for humanity."

Service is the word, too,
       at the Quaker school
as students prepare
       to re-build villages
after a Nicaragua earthquake.

——————————— ◆ ———————————

We are possibility.
       We are our becoming.
In the morning coffeehouse,
       there are greetings to a young poet,

and a dance professor,
       hellos to a circuit court judge.
A local artist swings by with a cup
       of Kenyan and we build the new or-
       der
from Jordan and Ganges and Yangstze.

In a single Fairfax County
        high school,
they speak one hundred
        and seventy-one languages.

If America is not a melting pot
        then maybe a cultural mosaic,
as the Canadians say.
        Then, there's Dizzy Gillespie,
African-American-Caribbean-world celebration.

In the morning deli,
        I munch a bran muffin,
over *The Washington Post*,
        blood and faith and terror.

In my rural town,
        hundreds of calls
pelt the women's shelter
        for domestic violence
amid auburn, autumn leaves.

I swirl a Guatemalan blend
        of coffee,
as good company one morning,
        as the traffic zips by.

A local artist displays
        her impressionistic
landscapes at the coffeehouse,
        frothy with color, azure, magenta,
dappled with bold yellow and gone purple.

———————◆———————

I draft a poem on a legal pad
        in the coffeehouse,
sipping a bottled water.
        A lawyer friend from Oxford

greets me with a big hello,
        carrying a dark roast
off to his office, as the sun
        splits a prism in the window.
A landscape on the wall glints with light.

I remember the black historian
        holding forth
at the Bahá'í Studies conference
        in Phoenix

and the black urban planner with her fine
        book.
This lovely, accomplished Bahá'í
        couple*, shining out, black folks
as "the pupil of the eye of mankind."

———————◆———————

Sometimes, this white boy
        just wants to step
outside the Anglo-Protestant upbringing.
        I want to go back

to the black gospel
        choir where I was the only white
and rock. I want to belt out
        God's thunder past credentials,
past control.

---

*Richard and June Thomas of the University of Michigan

As J.B. Phillips wrote,
        Your God Is Too Small.
Sometimes we may want to make
        God respectable and middle class.

I think we almost always
        want to make God agree with us.
Today, I want to let go
        of my idea of God
and find that horizon beyond the horizon.

———————————— ◆ ————————————

I read a map of the new world
        this week happening
into this one at the very official
        World Bank.

Bahá'í, Christian, Sufi,
Muslim, Jewish, Hindu, Buddhist
        and Jain, among other leaders,
meeting with the Bank president
to place values at the center of development.

148

Near the ocean one day,
     as my cousin and I
discuss the United Nations,
     I see the waves as relentless,

surging wisdom, need, answer, onslaught, res-
     tive bob and depth.
It is the unfinished business
     of God's creation
beyond all our books and thoughts.

The clouds are dark and nimbus, as the
     waves heave,
as we stand on the dock
     and gaze out toward the horizon.

The sea is fascination.
     It sighs, swirls and contains.
It is so very other.
     Each wave, frightens,
comforts, lulls.

Within this distant God,
        there is the nurturing One,
the God who seeks us out,
        even before we seek Him.

The Unseen Knower reaches
        down to us unbidden.
The firmament is there in the pitch
        of night. Always dawn
remembers us before we wake.

———————————◆———————————

I face the Big Empty.
        Deep Nihil, Drenching Dark.
Faceless masks. Doorways
with no knobs. Songs with no music.

I listen for what the last
        skylarks sang
in the last, wordless chorus
        of nowhere. At the end
of a copious absence. Deep Dream. Double Yes

From the Pit, to Surge
        with Being Itself.
Bahá'u'lláh, Buddha
        of Universal Tao.

Dharma Dram and Drum.
        It is a conviction made
solid to feel this living,
        sacred thing
deep down in the marrow.

———————— ◆ ————————

A Zen-Buddhist Quaker
        speaks on Interfaith Dialogue.
A world order scholar
        writes about a global people's assembly.

An attorney born in the Mexican-
        American barrio of Detroit
teaches conflict resolution
        at the Bahá'í school in Switzerland.
These shafts of hope are cast in the half-light.

"One world is all we have,"
        says one Harvard theologian.*
Amid magnolias and megatons,
        we must learn to forge

the bonds of peace, a tensile
        strength of bridges
that bear the weight of our
        all too human traffic.
Another way, toward healing.

———————◆———————

We need to move toward
        cultures of peace,
one continent without war,
        linked to the next.

Forgiveness can be a whole new
        heroism. Tolerance
can be the toughest thing to do
        sometimes. In Jerusalem, listening to
the Moslem call to prayer, the Jewish cantor.

---

*Diane Eck, Director., Religious Pluralism Project

The weather for change
        may be turbulent,
but it is the only front
        we have.

Interfaith dialogue
        in the Arab Quarter,
Muslim and Jewish moderates,
        listening to each other,
as a while new way of happening.

———————————— ◆ ————————————

I remember counting the waves,
        pulsing and relentless,
against the sea-walls
        of the prison-city of Akka.

Across the bay from Mount Carmel
        in Israel where the Spiritual Titan,
Bahá'u'lláh ruled from His solitary
        prison cell, under brutal conditions,
no food at all for days.

A Stanford biologist,
　　　a specialist in the brain,
says that religion clearly
　　　has some biological basis,

because it is occurring
　　　in our bodies, as such,
and happens across cultures.
　　　Our brains may be
"hard-wired for God."

As the world grows surreal
　　　with its blood and tasteless nights,
I take a breath on a dark evening
　　　and summon a dram of wonder.

I pivot on my walk
　　　and savor a slice of moon.
I drink the sloping hillsides,
　　　sip the skyline,
and say one more prayer for peace.

Past the iron-lung emotion freeze
        of the nuclear era,
my feelings strapped into my sides
        like ice, I nearly held my breath

for decades, waiting for the big up-ending,
        the big blow.
So far, the final obscenity
        has not blurted out and we have held
the game just short of checkmate.

In the landscape of the dire
        and the possible,
I dream toward the future,
        and pile the horizon with hope.

I solve myself in a calculus of wonder.
        In a dark time,
I am glad to see the sunburst dawn
        one more day,
And kindle spirit's fire anew.

The brick walkways
        in the Historic District
pass under my feet
        as memories of my own future.

I amble down the walking mall,
        toward the Handworks Gallery
with the global handcrafts,
        the Book Gallery and Deli-on-the-Mall,
used book store and coffeehouses and pubs and her.

———————————◆———————————

Red beans and rice,
        peppered up nice,
some Jamaican steel drum band,
        here in front of the 1840 Old Courthouse.

I piece together life and memory,
        like abstract expressionist efforts,
with a twenty-four hour train trip
        to the Quaker school and notes
to the deaf girl from Gallaudet, past the coal mines.

The Irish Lion Pub started
        to crank about nine.
The bartender came from Belfast
        and a guy at the bar saw me

writing poems on napkins
        even though I did not drink.
"A bottle of champagne for the house,
        if you can write one like Yeats," he said.
Twenty minutes later the bar toasted the poem.

———————— ◆ ————————

Today, while the sky still held
        high above continents and seas,
enormous armies yawned
        and dawdled away from their posts.

Today, warring religions veered out
        of each others' way
and doubled back to pray
        in each others'
churches, mosques and synagogues.

Globalization and terrorism
        heave into our lives,
helpless, imperiled, damaged
        by what we want.

Admen created wants where there
        were none, corporations
creating admen out of lit. majors.
        Some of us reel back into the past, or
With Trilling, "living between" as the only honesty.

———————— ◆ ————————

In the Shenandoah auroral sunset,
        a single figure
appears in front of the old Courthouse,
        setting up his microphone and amps.

Soon, he sings folk songs about coal miners,
        Vietnam, migrant workers,
like those on the edge of town, sweatshops
        and the sea. He regales us
with tales of the road, tracing the Valley twilight.

The brass quintet settles
        in the alcove of the college
 for a noontime concert, a rising
        are of clarion sound.

The surge of royal brass
        declaims democracy as Copland's
"Fanfare for the Common Man" sweeps down
        the corridor of the student center. The waves
of power argue the nobility of city workers.

Edging into the light,
        the sunburst fields
of the universal dream
        anoint us with their joy.

Cajun food or Indian
        before world music tonight
which will be Persian santour,
        Middle Eastern dumbek drum,
Ashante African flute and Japanese koto.

Past the rudderless dark,
        into the backlit space
where the weather for hope
        enfolds us with its dawning,

we churn past the driven storm
        of the drumming thunder
and begin the construction of base camp:
        new order. On the possible-mount we frame
a world law where love is the heart of the code.

———————————◆———————————

When the lights go out
        for the last time, I will be
glad to go where the fundamentalists
        are sure I am going:

that is with all the other Bahá'í's,
        Buddhists, lapsed Catholics,
humanists and reform Jews – folks
        with minds of their own. There, near
Nantucket-mind, we will sing on the cosmic rubble.

As a Bahá'í I join
        other progressive believers in moving
beyond the dogma of doubt,
        the church of despair.

Of course, it is very trendy
        to assume a mannered cynicism,
to believe in not believing,
        the jaded cloister.
Some people make a living at it.

We weep our silent tears
        as the Bahá'ís in Iran
remain very much in danger.
        A local Bahá'í of Persian descent

says letters back home
        even registered mail
are opened and censored
        violating all manner of international law,
Bahá'í children kept out of school.

We urge up and out
        toward a passionate world
culture, at once united yet
        diverse, from Kyoto to the Hague

to New Delhi to Kampala
        to Panama to New York.
Bahá'u'lláh, a fresh measure
        of spirit-fire: Resurgent Logos,
Buddha of the Planet-Walkers.

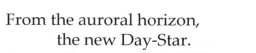

From the auroral horizon,
        the new Day-Star.
Avatar. Emergent possibility
        surges with leonine yes.

Over the dream-scape
        of the earth-long terrain,
we sing the new era
        and its hope-line,
dwelling down deep in that ground, that fixity.

Today, there is coffee
        with a Coalition
for Race Unity member
        and a veteran

of the War on Poverty from the 60s,
        A call to the Bahá'í
National Center finds Bob Henderson
        in, the second straight
African-American chief executive.

———————— ◆ ————————

With parents from New York
        and Boston, I joke
about there being ten liberals
        here in this Virginia town

and how we all know each other.
        Still, the gentle speech,
cordial and gracious, makes daily life
        a kind of dance,
from one bedroom to Federal mansions.

Somehow making music
        goes well beyond
"note-getting" toward
        relaxing into it,

instead of trying too hard.
        It is getting out of the way,
coming lightly over the top,
        not forcing your way up
for those high notes.

◆

A friend at a progressive
        think-tank in Washington
writes a book called *Global Dreams*
        nightmare multinationals –

financial predators.
        A friend at Princeton
however, sends articles
        about reining in the beasts
through world law.

Among Down Easters in Maine,
        there is a single road-sign
where one world comes to visit
        with actual town names off in every direction:

Norway, Paris, Poland, China, Peru,
        Limerick, Belfast, Athens, Moscow.
Then in Missouri, the world community finds:
        Cuba, Rhineland, Alhambra, Brazil,
Sligo, Warsaw, Vienna, Vichy and Versailles.

———◆———

On my way to class
        to teach contemporary poetry
I swirl a Costa Rican blend
        and remember that gem of Central
        America.

They have their earth-friendly
        policies toward the rain-forest,
a solid record on human rights,
        at the forefront of the peace movement,
healing herbs from the jungles.

As Mark Twain said,
     we write what we know.
Still, after twenty years
     as a Bahá'í, I do not know

the heart of 'Abdu'l-Bahá,
     such depth and range of spirit –
the Ocean of Bahá'u'lláh's
     Word and Power –
I watch from the shore in amazement.

———————◆———————

As a youngish poet and a Bahá'í,
     I so admire the Bahá'í Guardian,
Shoghi Effendi, for his literary skill
     and study at Oxford.

The Guardian was tough-minded
     and sensitive, spiritual
and decisive and visionary. We watch
     astonished at the arc of his life,
his trajectory toward the implicit future.

Adazzle, aswim, the lions
        of the new day, stagger
and roar, up-surge toward,
        sing and swing,

tuck and drive, past the automatic,
        the usual to those perfect spires,
those cedars of Lebanon,
        the cotillion Lovers of the New Yes,
succour, luck and graces, simmer, thin and trim.

———— ◆ ————

At the bagel place,
        I have a sun-dried one
with chive cream cheese
        and peach nectar iced tea.

The farmers' market up the street
        sells fresh cider,
produce of all types, walnut
        and zucchini bread,
even fresh fish off the Chesapeake Bay.

We stretch at the Interfaith
　　　　Conference tomorrow
to take in the expanse of Hindu,
　　　　Jewish, Christian, Moslem, Bahá'í,

Buddhist, Sufi and First Peoples.
　　　　We converge, diverge and merge
as the new era is born amid concord here
　　　　and blood and hope and rage
on the evening news. World citizens from soldiers.

———————————◆———————————

On the other side of war,
　　　　my mother sees unexpected friends,
When the world sees the pit,
　　　　she sees God at work in the aftermath.

When the losses weigh in
　　　　like shipwrecks,
she sends bulletins of hope
　　　　to the far corners of darkness. A Magel-
　　　　lan
of love, she discovers imperatives of joy.

Absolve, absolve, but remember too.
        The many thousand turns
of a decade reckon and forgive.
        Yet, the dead leaves on a hill

and the consecutive stars go on
        in silence, unrelenting.
A tree rises out of the ever-giving
        earth and its heaving.
A factory spews its promise, demand and threat.

———————◆———————

A cultural mosaic
        of spectral hues,
skylights of possibility
        on the Walking Mall

during the International Street
        Festival: the Greek Orthodox
Church selling Greek food:
        Soul Food from a Black church:
Vietnamese, Thai and even Country Cookin'.

Ascent on the path,
        may be followed by descent
yet, even here we can spiral
        in progress in our faith,

knowing that *Holy the Firm*,
        as Annie Dillard would have it
where even the pit is sacred.
        As in recovery, we recognize
that we must touch bottom and rise.

———————◆———————

Paul Tillich said that the fall
        of man was a fall upward.
Or *Falling into Grace*, as my friend
        Jay St. Rain has it.

We may need to learn how
        to blow it safely.
We may need to be able to
        take risks with a safety net,
to become humble by failing at humility.

We have entered the impossible
        land, that never-will-be
that is all around us,
        that post-analogue afterburn

where the outlandish DaVinci drawings
        of future flight
fill the sky with routine shuttles to New York,
        and supersonic test flight heroism
has become pretzels and first-run movies.

Uncivil man continues
        with his civil wars
despite a growing global sense
        of common sense.

The costly path to oneness,
        strewn with bodies and blood,
reminds us of how
        some insist on suicide bombers
and fighters instead of all hues at one.

At the Bahá'í Studies Conference
        in Tempe, near Phoenix,
Native Americans from Alaska
        chant and play their drums.

A Persian-American woman
        just out of the Wharton
Business School speaks about
        Business Ethics. Conversation
with a scholar from Berkley over pastries.

———————— ◆ ————————

Just over the Blue Ridge,
        I celebrate Jefferson
and Madison, with their freedom
        and federalism.

I reach back to Degandwidah
        and Pontiac, Iroquois chiefs,
who founded the federal ideal
        and Virginian Woodrow Wilson
who took it to the world.

After fighting with terrific heroism
        and horrendous losses in all-black troops
with white officers in the Civil War,
        black soldiers in the 1800s

were forced to serve only West of the Mississippi,
        in the most dangerous posts.
Fighting with worn out equipment but
        with great bravery, they were named
"Buffalo Soldiers" out of respect by the Indians.

The U.S. Marshal who caught
        the most outlaws turned out to be
African-American. The U.S. Government
        refused to allow blacks to serve in W.W. I,

so the French welcomed and honored them.
        "The Tuskegee Airmen" in World War II
never lost a single bomber under their protection
        even though the white hierarchy
thought they were not smart enough to fly.

Down the Shenandoah Valley
        to the Unitarian Church
where a friend is minister
        and there are readings

from the *Tao-Te Ching*, Gibran
        and the Indian poet, Tagore.
Later, Bahá'í Interfaith Devotions
        at the Quaker Meetinghouse,
then lunch at the Greek place, Up Valley Pike.

———————— ◆ ————————

A Lakota-Sioux flutist
        stops in town.
A Native American woman
        poet speaks of poetry

as "dream reason."
        She sees the layering
of many worlds beyond
        this shadow world,
to write poems as an act of love.

As I sit in the Bahá'í meeting,
  which we hold in the Quaker Meetinghouse,
I think of the ferry from Seattle
  to Vancouver Island.

I think of the shafts of light on the House
  of Worship outside Chicago,
from incidental music to a Shakespeare Festival
  in Stratford Connecticut. I notice a phrase
from *Rumi*, grazing across my mind.

Brother John, still in Washington, D.C.,
  an environmental lawyer,
providing oversight for the US
  Agency for International Development

and multilateral projects,
  such as those from the World Bank
and IMF – this week he's taking on Exxon.
  Nothing like small stakes.
John is helping bring the rule of law to the planet.

I range out across the miles,
        across the American continent,
only this time in a jet,
        instead of my old Chevrolet.

As Bertolt Brecht has said,
        there will still be singing
in the dark times, so I sing
        this earth and I sing America,
that we may all usher in "the Most Great Peace."

———————◆———————

Hear these calm, haunting
        choral meditations resonate,
with several from Rachmaninoff and
        Tchaikovsky, but not in the Western style.

America is a very young country
        and there are many hundreds
of winters in those chords and harmonies
        and darker days have come and gone
than we may well imagine.

Listen to the Russian Orthodox
  chant on Christmas Eve,
this deeply layered sound of sopranos,
  altos and tenors to be sure,

but oh, those double basses.
  Hear the centuries
reverberate down the halls
  of their iconic houses of worship,
back into the Byzantine Era.

A stonemason who carved
  a piece of the National Cathedral
speaks with me at a friend's
  art show as snowflakes fall outside

like distant cousins.
  They are such carvings themselves,
with such care evinced by the First Artist,
  etched into each mortal and ardent flake,
destined to weep away its brief, crystalline moment.

Outside, leaning against my car,
     I wonder about the human prospect.
We remain these ambient, three-dimensional ques-
     tions, happenings in bio-chemistry.

We may be God's letters to Himself and to us, que-
     ries against this huge backdrop
of billions of stars and deepest space.
What will our answer be on this precious planet, in
     this distant corner of the galaxy?

From
Work Songs
(2004)

Song for the Workers

For those who sweep up,
 for those who bend
and lift and carry –

we give homage here –
for the steady hand,
unnoticed – for those

who drill and apply
themselves to the hammer –
those who read the blue-

prints, housewives,
who have a job already,
and without recognition,

teach the next generation –
for those with trucks—computers—equations –
those with saws and levels and desk –

I give them homage here.

We, the Determined

A Poem for the Disabled

We, the determined, the broken,
the disabled cannot tell you
how to live your lives,
although the world's functionaries
    have plenty to say to us.

We may remember clear, lucid days
when minds or eyes or limbs
worked with clean, precious
clarity, or maybe the darkness
    has always been there.

Maybe the mind whirls
with its horrible half-functioning,
mocking us as we broach another day
with our words and our degrees
    and hopes not to stumble.

Friends from youth, no longer
friends, never real it seems have dropped
away, unable to face us, unable
to carry for a few brief hours
    the pain we carry every day.

Yet, we press on, knowing the family
and friends who do care, care
deeply, if awkwardly at first.
Dream on, friends, the going may be slow
    but we can do anything with enough time.

Each passing toll gate
must be paid with our
pain and grit and brains.
The heights are in us.
Press on.

On Light

I am thinking of things that are,
angels and workers and suns,
things that reach and find and become
sources and prisms and ways home.

a revered teacher can be this:
a schooner off the coast of Maine,
a farm or an art gallery,

things apart that join others,
choruses and symphonies,
things that fly.

I am thinking of perfection,
elegance and simplicity together,
the symmetry of time,
the auroral dusk on a New York skyline,
dawn over the Blue Ridge.

There Is a Seat at the Table

There is a seat at the table
for every Native American,
and every African; every Christian
and Jew and Moslem;
every refugee and
oppressed one; every sinner
among the hunt clubs, stockbrokers,
and the few; the cabbie,
the foreman and the farmhand;
the old crone and the old man
with his pet peeves; the rock'n'roll
divas and the mezzo-sopranos;
the jazzman and the Indian
classical sitar player;
there is a seat at the table
for the dispossessed of every continent;
for the peacemakers and the wounded;
for every linguistic group and every
language within them; for every shade
of brown, every orientation;
every worker and Brahmin;
for every nuance of intellectual
distinction; bring them on; there is room
for the human race in the human race,
all are one.

Rock Musician with a Ph.D.

My cousin, the rock musician, has a Ph.D.
and his girlfriend/vocalist calls him "Doc."
He does a book review now and then
when he's not watching MTV.

They play the Greater Boston clubs
and make good money on their dreams.
Ted is a traditional sort of guy, though,
likes the Boston Red Sox, even when they lose,
Jeffersonian humanism and Nat King Cole.

I have gone with them to the clubs
and disappeared like woodsmoke
into the dim lit room where paradise
was dancing music for now
and your own originals one day.

When I visit Ted, the leisure of much reading,
healthy food and a generous dose
of full-blown cynicism all are in the air.
Near the end of his Ph.D. in Political Science,
he sent up quantitative social science

with a piece called "A General Theory
of Santa Clause." The article published
in a major daily. His wit has driven
two VW buses over 100,000 miles each
and the '80s are still the '60s in his jeans.

Handworks Gallery Vignette

Another free-flying
Handworks Gallery day:
Maryam listens to folk tunes,

Sara shows an onyx ring,
Zulu baskets, Shenandoah Valley pottery,
kaleidoscopes that bend the mind,

a friend sculpts coffee tables
out of sheer hunks of wood,
Sallie's hand-painting of the planet.

Jazz Song

Sitting in the cafe,
listening to the blues,
reminds me of the Blue Wisp Jazz Club
     in Cincinnati,

taking in the club trio,
a piano man, bass and drums,
like the Ohio River running
     through your mind

rush, surge and whip—
no need to go to New York
to hear them, just sit there
     in the waves of sound.

later in the set, a sax man
joins them, lets the club rip
wide open—a bass player comes to mind,
     one who says

"Yeah man, I blow bass,"
as if his fingers were wind—
so I drive my feet to town
     after this.

best car I ever had, tickling myself
to hear Cincinnati Joe Duskin
fly off the poster at the Blue Wisp,
     dropping onto Martha's Vineyard,
     riding his piano.

World Music Medley

The salsa music invites
at the coffeehouse,
     barely 7 A.M.,
     even so

I remember the street band
playing mariachi in Santa Barbara,
     enchiladas
     at the Mexican place

for lunch with the founder of peace
studies at the Quaker school,
     former attorney
     for Cesar Chavez

the Farmworkers Union organizer, as well
At Wesleyan in Connecticut,
     I took in the Javanese Gamelan
     orchestra—indigenous players

in world music there—West African
drummers, Indian classical sitar,
     Greek dumbek players
     folk tunes from Eastern Europe,

Chinese, Japanese and Korean
court music intersect, early Celtic
     strains as bagpipes find their origin
     in the Middle East.

On Architecture

Notes on a Virginia Town

The only endowed public
high school in Virginia rises out of the hill
as a dream of the ancients:

columned frontage gives off
onto porticos and double-rows
of oak and cherry trees
on each side of the campus,

huge, columned Federal homes,
carved out of hillsides
in the Historic District
give tree-lined streets

their ambient splendor,
numbers of stone houses
boast of fields fertile
with stone and orchards,

past the Beaux Arts edifice
of the turn-of-the century
public library, so many
painted white brick places,

with dark shutters, leading to
522 North, with hedges
on each side, Victorian
homes, food for hungry eyes.

The Mind of God

With thanks to Stephen Hawking

From the big bang to black holes,
from the way things are
to why they are—Aristotle, Newton,
Galileo, and Einstein—Kant and Whitehead—

physicists and philosophers
describe an arc, the history
of time—delving into the big questions,
how we and the universe got here and why,

from waves to particles to relativity
wondering at last about the mind of God.

God, the Potter

I sit here on the edge of the
afternoon, reporting what God
seems to be about real-time
transformations,

working with matter, as a
potter works with clay,
signing each piece of work
with a touch of spirit

there He goes with another sun-shower.

The Luck of Flight

Deep in the soundless luck
of flight, at 30,000 feet,

a hermetic seal forms an envelope
of breathlessness—

you wait for the cloudless air
above the white tufts—

there is something heavenly about
watching patches of farmland

from the sky—you are lifted up
in your smallness—

dependent on aeronautics,
control towers and a crew

you don't know, the terror
becomes sublime—at one

with the beauty—you watch
descent eat up sky, and rivers

get larger, as the flight attendant
secures her belt—this is

a roaring that you do in place, a
confrontation with mortality itself

Loading Dock Blues

You show up early to put
    the previous day's
boxes in the incinerator—
    a choice job
in winter, yet, the smoke
    and ashes fly up
in your face, chastening you
    in your student's
poverty—even as you try
    to keep the heat
and light burning, embers
    and flames sending
you back into the stockroom
    shortly, the trucks,
eighteen-wheelers begin to show
    up, as you guide them
back, back, flush with the multi-
    layered, rubber pads
on the edge of the loading dock
    they settle in there,
and stop—the drivers and the stock-
    crew, all of you,
empty the whole truck, at least
    your portion of the load,
in minutes, piled high on your carts—
    as you wheel and pivot
away from the truck, with your load,
    a single NA brew after work,
    all you can afford.

From
Sonata of Spirit
(2005)

One Chord, One Song

From the court music of China
to Middle Eastern modalities –

from the call and response
of the spirituals to the chamber

music of Europe – from Micronesia
to Malaysia to the Solomon Islands –

the music of all is replete
with sonorities of spirit –

whole tones, half tones
and quarter tones – subdivisions

of pitch within speech itself –
how jazzmen and Indian classical

sitar players will improvise
for hours and bend their notes –

Tanzania home – South Africa home –
all the Americas, from the Aleutians

to Tierra del Fuego – the counterpoint
of all – one song, one chord, one chant –

one planet, whole and free.

River Song

After the Nile dreams Africa,
and the Hudson surges through
your improbable hands,

you wish the Shenandoah
into its curves,
and the Potomac curls

down those political miles
toward Washington –
the Charles floats its crew shells

and Eliot's sweet Thames
still streams along
with interwoven currents –

the Jordan, Ganges and Yangtse
run their forever course
with timeless blood and spirit –

then, the power-drive
Mississippi and Amazon
carve their continents

with heft and roll and steam.

Meditation Hall

A Bahá'í, a Christian,
and a Buddhist gather
at the meditation hall,

admiring the buttresses
and hardwood floors –
earth-tone pillows for sitting.

The hall embodies and uplifts
the spirit as your glance
follows the rising arc

of foot-thick wooden beams.
The patina of the floor
invites the gaze

to a shaft of light
that refracts and dances
at your feet. You lift

your heart to the great God
of all – as the Buddhists say
"the Unformed, the Unoriginated" –

the light is a music of the eyes.

The Colors of One Palette

In the lap of the Shenandoah Valley,
          there gather two Bahá'í artists,
a Unitarian minister, a liberal Baptist
          minister, two Catholic meditators,
a Zen-Buddhist Quaker professor – this joyous
          song of oneness in our speech, together –
a Native American named Phoenix, a Sufi
          named Sky – a Zen Master, Buddhist
monks in their saffron robes, Catholic monks
          as well, a Jewish Rabbi, in memory,
this roundness of spirit within spirit –
          boundaries dissolving with sheerest,
cordial feeling – lovely smiles in every corner
          of the conference room – an Islamic
M.D., a Bahá'í and a Christian, chatting
          in the line for vegetarian lunch –
a Methodist professor of religion is off
          to Cape Town, South Africa
to speak to the Parliament of World Religions –
          a Hindu Swami leads a meditation
as we join in the silence beyond words
          that speaks the Greater Tao beyond names –
a lavender sunset, a tincture of outlandish
autumn leaves – colors flare out in one palette.

The Heart's Own Currency and Cost

For Louis Gregory

An attorney, every chandeliered hallway
of Washington available to him –
a good town for black folks then,
    according to Dubois –

instead, Louis sought the incandescent
hallways of the infinite – instead
of the law firms, he stood firm
    in the covenant –

from the cradle of civil rights
to the cradle of the new world,
the whole trip, as the honored guest
    of the Master Himself –

Mr. Gregory treasured the inmost
law of love with his priceless dignity –
those inner laws of the spirit
    charmed him –

at last, not the world of codicils
and arguments at the bar – but the modest bill
of fare on the trains, the colored cars,
    Louis was "pure gold" said the Master –
    the heart's own currency and cost.

Rosette

For the Bahá'í women

A young Bahá'í woman, at the top
    women's school
Wellesley College, studying economics,
    joins with Christian,
Buddhist, Muslim, Hindu, Sikh,
    Native American
and African faith traditions
    to form a model
of campus, religious diversity.
    An internship
at the World Bank leads to work
    at the Bahá'í
World Centre, where she delves,
    excels
in the development field with
    trips into
the hands-on praxis of it all –
    education for
the young mothers in India
    and elsewhere –
at the World Centre, every sort
    of ambassador,
pilgrim, and journalist –
    a procession of gladness,
skill and caring – hospitality
    is Persian tea,
and the attar of rose, amid
    spreadsheets and chocolates.

Folk Song

She wears a peasant dress
      and a cotton vest
a friend made for her – we

join the folk dance group
      for some Israeli
line dances – then, off

to the walk out to the college-
      owned farm where
we will pick some vegetables

for the week – we play a bit
      of Dvorak, later,
the *New World Symphony*,

which borrows from American
      folk traditions,
even as he had become one of the first

ethnomusicologists, scouring
      Eastern European
melodies for his rhapsodies –

she ties back
      her hair in a bandana,
to pick beans from the French

      intensive beds
on the organic farm – work still to do –
      work still to do –

Farming Meditation

From his own cover crops,
intensive vegetable beds
and fields of grain, he formed

a new landscape in the world
and in the mind. the tall grasses
and the roadside fence posts

and telephone wires stretched
across the American Middle West
from the place like extensions

of his own hands. He dug
his honest post holes and
tamped them down and

mulled his cider with friends
in the delicious cool of fall evenings.
He trundled over the snow-covered

fields mid-winter and listened
to the hush and hum of their quiet.
His bending and his rising for a generation

forged an aching and a meditation.

Men's Song

for Dennis Grundman

The relentless luck
of God, the rise and risk
of men in kingship
adorned with their manes,
drum-songs, and queen-sake
      loves –

a work song, too, of going
out, away from the house,
from base-camp, from digs
all too promising and static,
      the daring

life of action, all too distant –
then, we take up our road-songs,
our loading dock blues, our hotel
nights, roiling on deadline –
      dawn on the construction site –

we take up our lives, and go
out into the midnight mist,
and sort through the thoughts
of God, the jasmine in our minds,
      and settle up – bring ourselves
      to account, and fruitage bring to bear.

Each Religion Is Larger than Itself

Each religion is
larger than itself,
pointing to the history
of religion – the quest
for meaning. A river

cuts out a valley,
a channel for its meanders –
it is by being that the river
offers water supply to
the towns nearby – why

empty longings, why forests
 become clearings for towns –
a wonder inside, a hunger
for the Great Being, an unnamed
yearning visits, and the Buddhas,

each, of the several religions,
visit us. Michael Ryan
names one of his books
God Hunger. You fill the void
as best you can – that is,

until "ultimate concern"* meets
the Ultimate, the Free.

---

*Paul Tillich's phrase for faith

204

A Credible Distance

A credible distance between here
        and the horizon's horizon
swirls with a darker cloud today.

We try to negotiate this car-bombed
        landscape, this desert
of the body politic – we plunge ahead.

The heat-hearted ways of these barren
        days will unsuit us
to easy praise but gain us hard-won solutions.

As Robert Frost said, "The shortest way
        around is through."
Muslims, Christians, Jews

and Bahá'ís kibbitz around the same table
        over vegetarian lunch
and the New World drives on, relentless.

Report from the Tao

A Buddhist monk seeks
you out at the bagel place,
a few hours off from the monastery.
Deferring to the saffron robe
and the tradition of the mendicants
you offer him a bagel with cream
cheese and chives – he accepts,
        bowing a bit –

your editor who lives in Geneva
and commutes to Oxford, England
as needed, to a distinguished
Bahá'í press, speaks to you
through those transatlantic
fibre optics, after singing
some Purcell – you mention playing
        a Purcell trumpet voluntary –

a liberal Christian friend puts you
onto a Catholic monk who knows
Wendell Berry, the poet, farmer,
teacher and essayist – fiction writer
too, with a collection of short stories
out called Fidelity – decades
with the same wife, his book of poetry
        The Country of Marriage
        strikes a chord.

Kent State Memoir

It is May, 1970 – the shots –
Kent State is a bit of history.

As soon as the news is news,
I am into the linen closet,

grabbing a huge black fabric –
the whole is cut that evening –

five hundred arm bands for them –
something in me felt the war

break that night – somehow it
hand ended in the national will –

three years to go, nonetheless,
I distributed the black emblems

at the traditional Virginia school
as precious tourniquets to it all –

something in the faces of my fellow
students registering the shock of it,

yet, an immediate assent, acceptance,
of the gesture, the only thing to do.

Politics at a Distance

I engage in politics by not going
        to Washington very often –
only as frequently as the bird within
        wants to sing a grand or laconic

or plaintive song for America,
        for earth – I meet with old friends,
the environmental liaison at
        the Bahá'í National Office –

or Dick, at the radical think tank –
        or Charles, at Brookings –
I go next door to the Institute where
        Dick works, and get some Greek food –

or meet with my brother, a long-time
        environmental man, an attorney,
an expert on endangered species
        and wildlife law – the White House

called him in to interview Bruce Babbitt
        for the post as Secretary at Interior –
yet, these things rest lightly on the heart,
        and I am back to the Valley in the same day.

"More Universal than Thou"

A Unitarian – a local architect –
and I spoke last night
about the several faces of
universality. I first noted

several Quakers I had known
Zen-Buddhist Quakers, agnostic
Quakers, or Christo-Centric –
all manner of people

expressing "ultimate concern" –
as the liberal theologian
Paul Tillich has said.
While acknowledging

the universality of Bahá'í
I joked, saying "We do tend
to be rather exclusive
about our universalities" –

we both laughed out loud
at this – Chuck offered
that Unitarians tend to be
intolerant of people who are

intolerant – this could be
called the problem of being
"more universal than thou" – or,
"the insider-universalists club."

Southern Moon

You order red beans and rice
at the cajun place a few paces
from the grounds at "Mr. Jefferson's
        University" –

"Virginia," as we know it – you
cross the Blue Ridge to catch
the leading environmentalist
        and Vice-President,

Al Gore, who opens a large, new
tract of land in Shenandoah National
Park – mail from the Carter Center
        in Atlanta

and the Southern Poverty Law Center
detail horrific hate crimes,
black church burnings, intolerance,
and genocide overseas –

there is beauty still, in azaleas
in Charleston, a walk to Washington's
headquarters, Stonewall Jackson's and
        Philip Sheridan's all on the same street,
        wisteria under a southern moon.

World Centre Vignette

In the lucid Israeli air
a gardener shapes and prunes
the cypress and the rose.

A brick walkway slices
the hedges amid pilgrims,
terraces and sheruts.*

The golden-domed Shrine
of the Báb, tipped in green
and red, floats on Mount Carmel

with regal providence.
Members of the Universal
House of Justice proceed

from their chamber
to welcome guests
with gravitas, warmth and grace.

Palm trees flare out
amid street sounds
of thrum and bustle –

Bahá'í World Centre hum.
The arc of luminous marble white
sails across the concourse of the eyes,
sculpting embodied Eden.

---

*Large Israeli shared taxis

For The Universal House of Justice

Mount Carmel Haifa, Israel

For that Seat of bold and luminous white
      cypress trees as lofted spires –
columnar, terraced lift – we tender honor here.

For that regal bearing, fused
      with democratic lights
cast upon our future history now –

each man of justice, emblem,
      bulwark, vow –
successive waves of statecraft,

suffused from that lustrous, marble site,
      pulsing toward
a commonwealth of earth

forming in this hour – those letters,
      text of Sacred Text –
we offer homage here – that imprint,
      indelible and free,
        O crux of world unity.

Prophet, Prisoner, Man of Peace

A dark, dungeon pit in the 1850s –
a Persian nobleman, in chains
    for his beliefs –

chanting choruses of prayers
with his fellows in a stirring
    new path –

thousands had surrendered
their last – each night, one more
    dances to his death –

the nobleman, Bahá'ulláh, survives
to dream that God will render Him
    victorious by His Pen –

the bastinado – exile over frozen
mountain passes – the stench of prison
    from Persia to Palestine –

nevertheless, hundreds and hundreds
of Tablets by His streaming Revelation –
    Prophet, Prisoner, Man of Peace –

honored by Tolstoy – honored
at last by governors, sultans, and clergy
    who opposed Him – today,
      His Word compasses the implicit globe.

To Learn and to Love

At the Bahá'í Studies Conference
      in Toronto,
the many faces of oneness – Persian,
      African,

Native American, Hispanic, Asian –
      Anglo as well –
all gather to cerebrate and celebrate –
      to learn and to love.

A scholar holds forth on the upward
      thrust
of the world commonwealth,
      wrapping

his mind around the sweep
      of history
with circumference, grace
      and power.

An international lawyer speaks
      of her work
in Africa, a judge runs workshops
      in conflict resolution from here to Burundi.

An economist lays out
      the early
circuitry of the emerging global economy,
      a physicist
unpacks the mystical roots
      of matter –
some say ninety per cent of all
      matter is invisible.

From the chandeliered ballroom,
        the hundreds
flow as one current into the hallway
        and its supernal lights.

On Einstein

"The most incomprehensible thing
about the universe is that it is
        comprehensible, Einstein once said –

"Time exists so everything doesn't happen
at once," he remarked – you can imagine
        God, the Unknowable Essence,

Foundation of all things, being delighted
to yield up the secrets of the heavens
        to this mystical physicist, so filled

with awe, quirky reverence, technical
brilliance, informed humility – there he is,
        Einstein sitting down for pastries
        and coffee with the Creator of the Universe.

Spading the Earth

Joined to the work, ground and firmament,
her own task, to settle
into it – spading the earth,

what was frontier,
farming the furrows
on a few organic acres –
solar panels for late fall

vegetables – a single cow
for milk – a few chickens
for eggs – she walks
a few miles to town –

trees hold hands across
old National Rd. Rt. 40 –
she walks on what was horizon –
this midwest soil – home enough

to be more than address for now.

A New World Song

We launch the new world
along the sky-dream
of the Ultimate Maker –

local blueberries blend
their way into muffins at a place
near the New Hampshire lake –

a blues benefit in the Valley of Virginia –
Bahá'ís and Unitarians sponsor courthouse
concerts on the Old Town Mall –

sister Jinny and her pediatrics
in the South Boston Health Center –
brother John with environmental oversight

of World Bank and IMF projects –
a friend from the experimental school in Vermont
teaching Hispanic kids in Chicago how to write –

the Native Americans tell us to "walk in beauty."

One Mosaic, One Mandala, One Home

Surely, all galaxies are explosively one,
      and the universe is kaleidoscopic,
and the God of all swirls, diversely one –

African and Amerindian and other
      first peoples surge toward
one mandala – from West African

to Creek-Cherokee to Oglala-Sioux,
      to the Pima of Arizona
and the Athabascan of Alaska –

one world – one home – out of the heat
      and geologic pressure of this hour –
from the "indigenous classical music

of America" that is jazz, to the origin
      of bagpipes in the Middle East,
to the first world music men,

Bartok and Kodaly, recording the folk music
      of Eastern Europe, we have
a mosaic of human cultures, multicultural windows –

from the Tao-Te Ching to the Bhagavad-Gita
      to the Upanishads to Bahá'í –
the Christ-Spirit present in all –
      the many faces of the trans-original Being.

Thunder, Dream and Harrow

Thunder, dream and harrow –
spring and draw and marrow –
the long-languid day is born

and God is etched in phoenix-
song – lunge toward your sites
of wonder – a slouch toward temple

church and mosque – find and father
forth, confer, demur and descend,
toward this footstool of your Lord –

this heat and hearth, this earth,
this prismatic, refracted
light – consent to join the dance

and no more cast asunder –
plow your heart and furrow
long the Day of God,

with penitents and the sod.

A Lake in the Mind

After a train trip up the East Coast,
back from Vermont, Amtrak lurch and jostle,
I pick up my car in Chevy Chase.

Past the pinball game of suburban traffic,
a lake in the mind caresses the frenetic
journey, rippling with light wind.

I trace the familiar undulations
of Rt. 50 outside the Beltway
past the estates of horse country.

I see that lake come into view
near the university on the edge
of town as students feed the ducks.

Past the Federal and Victorian houses,
Canada geese strut
by another freshwater dream
as white cumulus sail the sky.

The Landscape That Is Not There

For Charles Wright

In the absolute momentum,
the total immersion in what is,
        there is this distancing
toward a landscape that is not there –

        a kind of meta-landscape, where
the metamorphosis of the self
        into a flower, pure lotus, is
the best thing to hope for –

        you make these recommendations
in total seriousness,
        about tilting toward wisteria,
or taking on the dimensions
        of a hyacinth, and there is no going,
there is no staying,
        only being in the nowhere,
                not forgetting.

Chicago Song

She meets you at O'Hare –
herself, a beacon in your pressured life –
morning devotions the next day
at the Bahá'í House of Worship –
the gardens' amplitude and latticework
of the temple above, spirit-soaring –

then, a light-hearted touch
over breakfast with strawberry
cheese blintzes – a drive
to the Institute of Art to see,
savor, relish the Impressionists –
Renoir, Degas, Monet, Manet, Seurat –

you saunter past the Goodman Theatre
for a stiff walk to the Museum Campus –
Adler Planetarium, Shedd Aquarium and Field Museum –
you gather your energies in the café,
then take in the natural history at the Field –
a deep drink of Chicago skyline with the Sears tower –

a walk through Grant Park where
jazz, blues and Chicago Symphony concerts
suffuse the air in season –
deep dish pizza for dinner – then,
Kingston Mines -- #1 Blues Bar at 9 –
once around Wrigley Field on the way –

"The Magnificent Mile" on Michigan Avenue
back up from downtown – upscale shopping
at Marshall Fields, Filene's Lord and Taylor,
and Cartier – back to Lake Shore Drive
which becomes Sheridan – lights from the temple
on the perfect black sheen of the lake.

Pin-Light Angels Amidst the Unspeaking Dark

You affirm, testify, obey, witness
            and affirm again, in matters of faith –
you assuage the outcroppings of doubt,
            the promontories of almost –

in those private places, those alcoves
            in the dark you let no one see,
even God, or so you think – there,
            you imply to some friend

that it is not all light here,
            even as the opaque nowhere within
expands amid the grind of meetings,
            the obdurate canvas of night –

even so, a wisp of evening pulls you
            to a window where the star-shine
ceiling on what is, scintillates with pin-light
            angels, amidst the unspeaking dark –

the deep unknowing, this empty conch
            of galaxy, still reverberates
as you listen to the billions of atoms
            vibrate and echo within.

Of Evergreens and Snows

A congress of conifer
gathers on the hillside
tucked in place
by a roughly spaced
ambient row of stone.

As the hill recedes behind
the grove, above and out of reach,
the nestled evergreen
remind this ripening soul
of winter nights and snows.

More than once, the heft
of weighty storms
pummeled the house.
One time in Maine
we children woke

to snow so high
we could not tell
where the cars were,
but we could sled and ski
with ease out our

second story window.
No joy greater for a child
than to shuttle from
house to twenty-foot drifts
and nearly walk upon the air.

The New Hampshire Lakes Region

The New Hampshire Lakes Region
heals the eyes with lucid dreams,

with evergreen landscapes
of spruce and fir and balsam,

these trees that fleck and flesh
the White Mountains and

the perfect crystalline blue
of the gorgeous lakes themselves.

This mosaic, this music of
spirit made physical,

this notation of the divine,
miles of avatar aqua,

manifesting the Unknown,
writing the script of the Unseen.

The weathered wharf by the cove
and old family cabins rest

as we slide the kayak into the lake
and trace the life force

in the immediate water itself –
the loons calling across the miles.

Witness

You affirm the lavender sky,
the oracular auburn brush strokes
      of the First Artist –

you witness to the universal dream
embedded in the conch, the wood-grain,
      the cedar of Lebanon –

drift and drive, the sea with its
churning, pounding, turning
      relentless tide –

from the improbable thrum
of the night-waves, you hear
      at last,

in your cabin, you know this
all could not be merely random –
      whatever

others may affirm,
you listen to your own soul, and hear
      the Blessed, Blessing Unseen, within.

A History of Dreams

You drive the ribbon of road
that is Rt. 50, past the quilt-work
farms and over the Blue Ridge
after a daytrip to Washington.

You confess the lofted grandeur
of the mountains to your God
as you note the clouds, cumulus
and tufted, drifting along the sky-road.

Then you sweep and surge
toward the history of dreams
that is the Shenandoah.
You break for Winchester,

sip and savor a cup of java
in an Old Town coffeehouse
as you chat with a Black principal
from the local high school.

That luminous temple of knowing
is floated on a hill, overlooking the city,
with its classic columns
and stately trees in double rows,

arrayed on the front campus,
honor guard for a gentler vision at peace.

In the Dance

You wander into the day
and fuse your longings
with the sun-shot afternoon.

You anchor your hope-line
maybes with that seascape
ark of earth headed out

toward its Luminous Self, then pray:
O Double-Dream, God-Man,
Exile and Man of Peace, dream us

homeward from our own private
exiles in our impossible lives
send down Your plumline

in our unlikely river-souls,
inscape, tendrils, inclining toward
Your heft of history –

O Lord, draw us toward a worthy dream today!
unfurl, unfold in each step,
some touch of peace to stay –

a word touched by kindness –
an insight free of blindness –
some highness in the dance –
blessed by Your own glance.

Why?

Because the state of Maine
burgeons with blueberries –

because my brother is hanging
tough as an environmental lawyer –

because the Blue Ridge rests
like a saddle for the sky –

because she is bright and
gorgeous and kind – and

a folk song slices the air –
because the night sky is honest

as midnight – because my old Royal
still taps out these bulletins –

because the Afghan place and
the Korean place serve good food,

here, where the Blue Ridge
and the Alleghenies cradle

the Valley of Virginia –
because the moon sits on the sky

like a saucer – and the winter
air is crisp tonight, like morning.

Tracings of Spirit

I imagine this – imagination being
      as genuine as sound –
that Israel is-real – that spirit is
      tracings of "being-becoming-itself" –

that the architects of all religions
      give blueprints, steps,
steppingstones – linkages – spiral
      ways of happening into
the next urgency – ladders to the next
      vivid way home –

that all the great Buddhas, the Gautama,
      the Christ, and all the others,
re-double our energies, urge and
      surge the river-Tao that is ours to live –

An Arts Suite

Ballot

For Jeanie Bauserman

This year, I vote
for the ash and linden trees,
the boxwood shrubs, the magnolia,

the blacksmith, the curator,
the music of motherhood,
I vote for the pylons of fathers,

the man in the turban,
the sitar player,
the Nigerian drummer,

a country walk, a walking mall
in the center of town,
the orchestra players,

the Javanese gamelan players,
I vote for bicycles, literacy,
the house husband,

the Native American flute players,
 thousands of service workers,
each one honed in their hours.

Buddhist Economics

For E.F. Schumacher

Two local poets scribe
away at the bagel place –

two local women have graduated
from the Naropa Institue –

the Jack Kerouac School
for Disembodied Poetics –

the farmers' market stands
open, with cider and vegetables –

two coffeehouses suffice us
with Costa Rican coffee and

Swiss chocolates – at dawn,
you write in your perch

as a dance professor friend
breezes by to pick up morning

coffee – you think of Bewley's
in Dublin, before your reading –

the Bahá'í school in India
teaches village agriculture –

late into the night, you
tap out these bulletins –

Bookseller with Coffeehouse

For Lorne Bair

A reckless amount
     of love
sips, cajoles, the
     rare book-
seller in the form
     of a new
computer that does
     book searches
for free. A coffee
     bar grows
out of his improbable
     mind, and used
books, too, extend
     from his arms
out onto hundreds of
     shelves. He
orders new books, swift,
     neatly packaged,
top quality only. After
     hours, he is
nestled in the rear with
     a world atlas,
counting the continents
     he holds within
the globe of his lucent brain.

Concert Zen

You lean into your part
      in life's symphony
with Concert Zen – acute,
      focused, engaged –

you anticipate, obey
      the conductor's baton –
you listen for your part
      in the ensemble –

as Dizzy Gillespie said
      of be-bop, you play
so everybody else sounds good –
      no matter how minor

the part, the playing needs to be
      musical – you demand of yourself
an attentiveness that is prayer –
      rehearsal sense in the every day –
      solo or not, to make music is worship

Kind of Blue

Thanks to Marvin "Doc" Holladay

The Ellington-Gillespie-Mingus saxman
　　　　and I cruise past the palm trees
near the South Carolina coast, away from
　　　　the Battery and its historic Georgian mansions.

Listening to Ellington's Far East Suite
　　　　and then Miles Davis' Kind of Blue,
we churn the miles out to the cypress
　　　　and marshes in the rural inland.

At a high school there we do our workshops
　　　　for the all-Black student body,
such sweet-tempered kids, their dark skins
　　　　traced by gleaming smiles.

We stop for Greek food back in Charleston,
　　　　and later, Japanese for dinner.
A reading for the Bahá'ís touches
　　　　the heart with a glistening dew.

Each Note, A Pearl

For my sister, mezzo-soprano, M.D.

Each note a pearl,
as some musician friends
have said – and so they
are, so the notes emerge
in their incandescent arc –
my sister is singing –

there, in the auditorium
at Brandeis, outside Boston,
her mezzo voice, tailoring,
evoking these visitations
to Handel, Purcell and Rorem –

each with their own peculiar
demand – each piece, offered with
delightful mastery, put across to the audience,
with especial presence, out to the last row

where I hear the Roethke poems
delivered with *sprezzatura*, with joy –
conversation between the poet,
composer, singer and audience –
the transaction is perfect, complete –

friends from the hospital where she is
a pediatrician, friends, who did not know
        she sang at all, pinned to their seats.

To Play With Feeling

You engage with two fine musicians
at the tavern with its rustic
rough-hewn tables,
over non-alcoholic brews.

The old jazzer formerly
of the Ellington, Gillespie and Kenton bands,
and the young conservatory trumpet
and wind ensemble professor –

they both yearn for the old days
when there was less "note-getting"
and more music played with feeling –
maybe less technical brilliance

but more musicality – the sparkle
 in the old sax player's eyes
tells of decades of playing with real soul –
the trumpet man tells of his teacher

leaving the great Cleveland Symphony
because it simply stopped being
fun anymore – no longer making music –
the three of you toast the flames

in the November fireplace
and head into the night
where the firmament
swirls with choreographed, star-light angels.

The Tao of Music

Breath is the foundation
of good playing – formative,
crux, crucible, matrix –

the instrument, whether voice or wind,
crucial friend, yet almost incidental
to the flow of air –

musicianship is meditation –
the Catholics would call music
"centering prayer" –

in the studio, with the master
teacher – an attitude of respect
as necessary component of learning –

music is a way of being –
the breath is sacred –
anatomy is emblematic –

from the abdomen to the throat
to tongue to forming the word "awe"
with the mouth – all, the Tao of Music.

For Love of Writing

In the schoolyard, in
the Afghan place,
in the Indian restaurant,
I write. Over the hill,
in the parked car, in
the cafe, in the coffee-
house, in the fast-food
joint, in the taco place,
in the family restaurant,
in the bar, in the library,
I summon the muse. In the
everywhere and the no-
where, in the hayloft,
in the temple ground,
in the Quaker meeting
house, in the church,
the back row, in my bed,
in the university chapel,
in the synagogue, I write.
In the Buddhist monastery,
and the meadow, and the forest
with their encompassing
light, I write. On dockside,
in the diner, and the tavern,
I write for love of writing,
        I write.

The Uses of Art

What use art? A stretcher
to wheel in the wounded –

a monument of blossoms –
a bit of latticework on the temple –

each painting, a record of a psychic diver –
each poem, an artifact –

life to be lived as a symphony or
maybe just some chamber music for the few –

each breath, a brush stroke –
each day, a dance.

Star-Road Universe

This universe and its star-road
for billions and billions
of outlandish eons, expanding
itself, breathing itself

into its elliptical, soul-self,
its illimitable, gorgeous-hearted spin –
This orb-tending, ordering,
relentlessly prismatic,

kaleidoscopic, how-about-those
lions-at-the-New-York-Public-Library –
centripetal-centrifugal-sea-turtle-
laying-those-eggs-deep-in-the-beach –

This musical-mystical-mathematical
roaring, resistless,
tectonic, consummate conundrum,
brain of God.

Soul-Song

You sail your car
around the Rt. 37 by-pass
along the orchards –
peach and apple –
you have known
since your teens.

down Rt. 11, the same
rough path, Valley Pike,
that the Union general
took for his famed
"Sheridan's Ride" –
turning the tide of the war.

tonight, under a luminous
set of stars, an orchestra
of angels, and a baton of moon,
you listen to the solo sax
of your Ellington-Gillespie-Mingus
friend Doc Holladay explore

his themes with feeling –
technique as a window on soul.

Elegy for Our True Brother

November 4, For Shoghi Effendi,
Guardian of the Bahá'í Faith

The Guardian, Pilot of the Planet
Project, Earth becoming Itself,
     has entered forever. An ache
in the body politic has gaped
     open, sundered, wound
     impossible to suture or to heal.

The world commonwealth that sprung
from his visionary mind
     rests in our hands to build
but was his to launch. The sacred
     progeny of his perfect pen
     render service still

even in his copious absence.
Leader, planner, translator, writer,
     designer, gardener –
all delivered with such grace,
     passion and power –
     let our efforts be our tears.

Last Words

Beethoven, long deaf, yet
brilliant, nonetheless,
said, "I will hear in heaven."

On his deathbed, Thoreau
was asked if he did not want
to make his peace with the Creator.

"I am not aware that we ever
quarreled," he replied. Voltaire,
an outspoken skeptic, said "My God."

Another Way

Moments into the city,
and you see her, daughter
of Hispanic and Anglo –

another way, beyond blaming –

a Black soldier in Kosovo,
a peacekeeper with two elder
Kosovo women, hugging –

another way, toward healing –

in Northern Ireland,
and in the Middle East,
longtime enemies, talking –

another way, beyond blaming –

moments into the city,
Native American drums,
Mexican silver, African flute –

another way, toward healing.

A Sonnet of Hope

We dream toward our lives, horizons piled
with hope. We consecrate our days with joy
toward some prospect of bonding pulsars,
and solve ourselves in a calculus of wonder.

We summon hope, and hoping summon good,
that in our time, the peace will deepen;
the deeper in our hearts, the dearer still
to shepherd, cultivate and cherish ever.

The honors of this service, like your embraces,
drift in and out of light as fire flips in sight.
We honor and befriend, drive and list
as oarsmen of the kingly ark befit the right.

So go immortals, into that bold night,
And kindle spirit's fire, in circuits bright.

Glimpses of Peace

A Palestinian Christian child
attends the Quaker school
on the West Bank –

an Irish poet, a Nobel
Laureate, writes poems
about his home in Balfast –

the Bahá'í World Centre
boasts gorgeous gardens
in December, on Mount Carmel –

a friend of mine splits
time between teaching
Peace Studies and pursuing

development work in Chile –
local people gather food
for those in need –

the white pin lights
on the Old Town Mall
accentuate the season –

through the mist, a single star.

Anyone, From Any Direction, Is Welcome Here

Bahá'í House of Worship Wilmette, Illinois

The House of Worship outside
Chicago stands aloft, an instructor,
a professor, exemplar of how to be.

This structure, latticework,
rising dome, buttresses, bulwarks,
steadily lifted staircase

in a continuous circle, all
around this saint in stone,
this hails a continent

to the ways of God.
Mostly the work of early
Bahá'ís in the West,

stories of their numbers
during the Depression
skipping lunch, and sending

those dimes and quarters
to the building fund.
Prayers said under the breath

in this space soar
with accurate wings
        to a most perfect, lighted
        curve of ceiling, or out
        to the gardens, nine walkways,
        nine portals, anyone,
        from any direction, is welcome here.

Go Deep

We honor the spirit
of the new era,
with its physic
and physics of love –

we include all hues,
and delight in the turnings
of mind – we affirm
the heart's effusions,

however coarse or fine –
we explode all assumptions
made of money only –
then, we go deep, go clean,

go true, right to the bone.

A Turn of the Clock: One Day at the Bahá'í Studies Convention

The first woman dean of an American
law school, now a Federal Appeals
Court Judge, speaks of conflict resolution –

Native people from Alaska drum, sing,
speak the sacred lore – how Bahá'í
holy writ helps renew their culture –

a black man and white woman
portray an early interracial couple –
a Persian musician sings her eloquent modalities –

three sociologists discuss
poverty and wealth, status and oppression
in the hotel lobby till 3 a.m.

What Purpose Faith?

to move the inner person
and the world toward
their own implicit, emerging
shape, toward peace –

to commit, to console,
to find our touchstones,
anchors, fence posts
on our journey – to commune

with life force, Essence,
God and each other –
to feel the "inner light"
in our inmost selves

and to see it in others –
to loft our hearts to always.

Windows on Being

A stonemason, carving a figure on the National Cathedral –
a carpenter, pouring himself into some artful trim –
a bricklayer, evening off a layer of mortar –
a composer, going over an orchestration –
a doctor, gazing at a patient's chart –

a Jew, at the Western Wall –
a Muslim, at the El-Aqsa Mosque –
a Christian, at the Church of Bethlehem –
a Bahá'í, at the Gardens on Mount Carmel –
an agnostic, under a throng of stars –

a physicist, with *A Brief History of time* –
a photographer, with a time-lapse sequence of the seasons –
a reporter, with what happens after the press conference –
a librarian, with access to worlds of meaning –
a prophet, with insight into the mind of God.

From
A New Era Symphony
(2014)

Song of the Planet

I sing of the planet
rimmed with light

the Untrammeled, the Unconditioned,
and a horizon of possibility.

A classical Indian sitar
player improvises for hours

and the Native American flute
and West African drum players

celebrate the coming and
going of day.

Deep into the evening
I listen to Chopin Nocturnes

or Bach keyboard suites
 and reflect on the day

as the music pours over me,
and lean toward the auburn dawn.

The Global Becoming

Thrust into the vortex
of the global becoming
and the old order passing,

you lift your days
to the God of all faiths
and dream a new thing.

Whether a call to Geneva
or to Canada or to Equador,
all dear Bahá'í friends,

or the dignity of indigenous
peoples in their native garb
from Africa to Latin America to South Asia.

Lucent joy and the work of it
spins you out for hopes
to help with climate change and more
counting each day as a gift, from God.

Matisse and Picasso for an Hour

As the world wrestles with
car-bombs, suicide attacks
and climate change, I go
to a Matisse and Picasso,
      and other Modernists show
      with my dear sister.

An hour of concentration
in the special collections room
      with the line drawings,
blue period landscapes,
and cubist delights of Picasso,
      as well as Matisse portraits,
      all lift and steady my heart.
My M.D. mezzo-soprano sister
is here for one of her regular visits
from Boston as a boost to my aging parents
and me. And indeed she is. I finish the viewing,
      with a glimpse at two-miniatures
      a Marc Chagall and a Paul Klee
both leaving the feeling of such
delight, such whimsy,
even in a dark time.

Global New Real

The new real, transcendent,
      tumultuous, unfolding,
contained in its own wisdom,
yet, unleashing its power by turns.

Luminous, trans-ethnic,
global new real,
      liberates self with Self.
Praise to Him Who is
Architect Of The New Order.
      King, Archer, Source.

Renewal of Faith

The elusive light of evening
      drifts off
into the nowhere of a misting
      dream.
The aching dark must be pulled
      back to
some sense of illumined choice
      and steady surety.
Lucent love and its necessary
      courage
will lead the keeping of the light
      in the lamp of civil life.
The renewal of faith
      achieves this
through the New Era
      and its Spirit.
Together we build the planetary DNA.

Race Unity at Five

At the age of five, I sat
on Lee's lap after spotting
cars as they passed by
our family's half-way house as we often did.

Lee was a black social work intern
unable to get housing anywhere else
in our 1950s town, so
he boarded happily with us.

That afternoon I stood
on Lee's lap and asked him
"Are you black on the inside too
or are you pink like me?"

He opened his mouth wide
so I could see and I looked
and exclaimed "Pink,
on the inside, just like me!"

Green Poem

A massive oil spill
off the Gulf Coast,
the worst environmental
disaster in American history.
Some of it may never
      be cleaned up.

China builds four or five
coal-fired power plants
per week. It also leads
the world in fossil fuel
emissions. Yet it also leads
      in production of solar collectors.

Climate change; climate ethics;
      a transformational nexus.
Sustainable development, renewables,
      Spiritual renewal and other new ways
of thinking will be needed to save our planet.

Peace Poem

A once and present
      hope I offer,
that somehow, possibly
      by will of wiser heads,
we come to peace,
      even if by weariness of war,
then, to resolve to lay down arms
      and take up
peaceable tools.

Then, I hope we incline
      the ear and heart
to new songs from all quarters
      that war itself
may become a distant memory.

Love Is the Way the World Opens

Love for God,
so much the way
the world opens
and becomes more itself,
is the way I make
the days livable as well.
The mention of God,
steadily on my breath,
as frequent as a glimpse
at evergreens
or the roadside grasses,
harmonizes the inner and outer way.
Sheer gratitude for a good meal
at the Indian place, then
back home for evening classics
tucking in at midnight to
Bach's cello suites,
exploring the range of the human soul.

Mercy-Blankets

Deep under consciousness,
      there, where the storm is not,
      where obligation ceases,

mercy-blankets are handed out
      for the wounded of the every day –
      to give the shock of it all a bed –

here, limpid waters pass over them,
      and color bathes them in delicious light –
      this is once and for all, a haven –

this semaphore of love, this ward
      for the broken, is a gift
      wrought from curses – a way to bliss.

On J.S. Bach

the Bach cello suites
      engage and explore
the very depths of
      the human soul as well as
the full range of the lovely cello.

Bach's Mass in B minor and
      St. Matthew Passion
are both monuments to his devotion and genius.
      The Brandenburg Concertos
are like old friends when played
      on period instruments.
The Well-Tempered Clavier
      and other keyboard suites on piano
when well-played, make my soul dizzy
      with delight, as if the celestial spheres
      had been clicked into place.

One with the Road

Driving on sheer ice –
this is a time for relaxed concentration –
a time for deliberate insecurity –
a time for Bahá'í Zen –

you drive with the road –
you listen to the winter quiet
and become one with the road –
you are more definite, yet

somehow less so – practical,
more involved, yet detached –
the rise and release of tension –
a lower center of gravity –

hugging, shaped to the road –
contoured into each curve –
a bliss and ease of not knowing –
acceptance of the possible –

present to the threat in front of you,
on toward your destination.

How Trees Vibrate

The trees vibrate today
with a lucid resonance –
there is something wholly adequate
about spring, today –

the main task for trees is to be –
being a tree, for them,
remains consummate wisdom –
it is a particularity for hard-boiled iconoclasts,
tough-minded realists, revolutionaries,

environmentalists, romantics, and
God-fearing Christians
who want to see a crucifix straight on –

above all, a tree, today,
makes ground by standing silent –
after all these centuries,
trees mean something still.

Logos and the River

There is a view of logos,
that places it in lotus,
that places it in a tree,
that places it in the river –

I am going to watch a sunset,
how the sky is sprayed with
a roseate gloss, tossed like paint –
there is something perfect in everything.

The Sound of the Human Voice

At the long light of sunset,
and into the deepest dark of night,
there is nothing so compelling

as the sound of the human voice –
familiar, fresh, raspy, singing,
crackling, chanting, intoning –

this music is close to the spirit –
it resonates with what is finally human –
the way the varieties of us speak

comes close to saying how
we feel, wish, hurt, dream and love –
I think it was Faulkner who said
after the world ends, people will go on talking.

Note to the Reader

I sing these songs
from the vortex,
from the placeless urge,
from the drive to go on

somehow to rise up
amid the current darkness,
somehow to say "Yes!" –
yes to the future within the present,

yes, to Bahá, to singing,
yes to the inexorable drive toward peace.

— **Michael Fitzgerald**

Made in the USA
Columbia, SC
04 June 2018